# DRIVE TIME
# SPANISH
## DELUXE PACKAGE

BEGINNER-ADVANCED LEVEL

Please Do Not Use This
Booklet While Driving

# LIVING LANGUAGE®

Published in the United States by Living Language, an imprint of Random House, Inc.

www.livinglanguage.com

Editor: Christopher Warnasch
Production Editor: Carolyn Roth
Production Manager: Thomas Marshall
Interior Design: Sophie Ye Chin

First Edition

ISBN: 978-1-4000-0656-4

Library of Congress Cataloging-in-Publication Data available upon request.

This book is available at special discounts for bulk purchases for sales promotions or premiums. Special editions, including personalized covers, excerpts of existing books, and corporate imprints, can be created in large quantities for special needs. For more information, write to Special Markets/Premium Sales, 1745 Broadway, MD 6-2, New York, New York 10019 or e-mail specialmarkets@randomhouse.com.

PRINTED IN THE UNITED STATES OF AMERICA

10   9   8   7   6

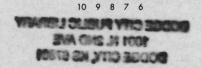

# ACKNOWLEDGMENTS

Thanks to the Living Language team:
Tom Russell, Christopher Warnasch, Nicole Benhabib,
Suzanne McQuade, Shaina Malkin, Elham Shabahat,
Linda Schmidt, Alison Skrabek, Carolyn Roth,
Sophie Chin, and Tom Marshall.
Special thanks to Agustina Carando.

# CONTENTS

**SUPPLEMENTAL VOCABULARY LISTS**     **79**

**GRAMMAR SUMMARY**     **95**

# DRIVE TIME

# SPANISH

## DELUXE PACKAGE

BEGINNER-ADVANCED LEVEL

# ON RAMP TO SPANISH

**Mile One**

| | |
|---|---|
| a car. | un coche. |
| It's a car. | Es un coche. |
| It's a big car. | Es un coche grande. |
| It's a small car. | Es un coche pequeño. |
| It's a new car. | Es un coche nuevo. |
| It's an old car. | Es un coche viejo. |

**Mile Two**

| | |
|---|---|
| a van. | una camioneta. |
| It's a van. | Es una camioneta. |
| It's a big van. | Es una camioneta grande. |
| It's a small van. | Es una camioneta pequeña. |
| It's a new van. | Es una camioneta nueva. |
| It's an old van. | Es una camioneta vieja. |

**Mile Three**

| | |
|---|---|
| What is this? | ¿Qué es esto? |
| Is it a car? | ¿Es un coche? |
| Is it a van? | ¿Es una camioneta? |
| Yes, it's a car. | Sí, es un coche. |
| Yes, it's a van. | Sí, es una camioneta. |
| No, it's not a car. | No, no es un coche. |
| No, it's not a van. | No, no es una camioneta. |

**Mile Four**

| | |
|---|---|
| What do you see? | ¿Qué ves? |
| I see a highway. | Yo veo una autopista. |
| I see a bus. | Yo veo un autobús. |
| I see a house. | Yo veo una casa. |
| I see a big house. | Yo veo una casa grande. |
| I see a building. | Yo veo un edificio. |
| I see a big building. | Yo veo un edificio grande. |
| I see a sign. | Yo veo un letrero. |

| | |
|---|---|
| Do you see a new car or an old car? | ¿Ves un coche nuevo o un coche viejo? |
| Do you see a big van or a small van? | ¿Ves una camioneta grande o una camioneta pequeña? |
| Do you see a big house or a little house? | ¿Ves una casa grande o una casa pequeña? |
| Do you see a big building or a small building? | ¿Ves un edificio grande o un edificio pequeño? |
| Do you see a new bus or an old bus? | ¿Ves un autobús nuevo o un autobús viejo? |

## Mile Five

| | |
|---|---|
| What is it? | ¿Qué es? |
| It's a car. | Es un coche. |
| Do you see a car? | ¿Ves un coche? |
| Yes, I see a car. | Sí, veo un coche. |
| Is the car big or small? | ¿El coche es grande o pequeño? |
| The car is small. | El coche es pequeño. |

| | |
|---|---|
| The car is white. | El coche es blanco. |
| The car is black. | El coche es negro. |
| The car is blue. | El coche es azul. |
| The house is red. | La casa es roja. |
| The house is green. | La casa es verde. |
| The house is yellow. | La casa es amarilla. |
| The house is brown. | La casa es marrón. |

## Mile Six

| | | | |
|---|---|---|---|
| a car | un coche | the car | el coche |
| a van | una camioneta | the van | la camioneta |
| a building | un edificio | the building | el edificio |
| a house | una casa | the house | la casa |
| a bus | un autobús | the bus | el autobús |
| a sign | un letrero | the sign | el letrero |
| a highway | una autopista | the highway | la autopista |

**Mile Seven**

| | |
|---|---|
| *The car is small.* | El coche es pequeño. |
| *The van is small.* | La camioneta es pequeña. |
| *The car is new.* | El coche es nuevo. |
| *The van is new.* | La camioneta es nueva. |
| *The car is old.* | El coche es viejo. |
| *The van is old.* | La camioneta es vieja. |

| | un... | una... |
|---|---|---|
| *white* | blanco | blanca |
| *black* | negro | negra |
| *blue* | azul | azul |
| *red* | rojo | roja |
| *green* | verde | verde |
| *yellow* | amarillo | amarilla |
| *brown* | marrón | marrón |

| | |
|---|---|
| *The van is white.* | La camioneta es blanca. |
| *The house is white.* | La casa es blanca. |
| *The car is white.* | El coche es blanco. |
| *The sign is white.* | El letrero es blanco. |
| *The van is black.* | La camioneta es negra. |
| *The highway is black.* | La autopista es negra. |
| *The sign is black.* | El letrero es negro. |
| *The car is black.* | El coche es negro. |
| *The van is blue.* | La camioneta es azul. |
| *The house is blue.* | La casa es azul. |
| *The bus is blue.* | El autobús es azul. |
| *The building is blue.* | El edificio es azul. |
| *The van is red.* | La camioneta es roja. |
| *The house is red.* | La casa es roja. |
| *The sign is red.* | El letrero es rojo. |
| *The car is red.* | El coche es rojo. |
| *The van is green.* | La camioneta es verde. |
| *The house is green.* | La casa es verde. |
| *The car is green.* | El coche es verde. |
| *The bus is green.* | El autobús es verde. |
| *The van is yellow.* | La camioneta es amarilla. |
| *The house is yellow.* | La casa es amarilla. |

| The building is yellow. | El edificio es amarillo. |
| The bus is yellow. | El autobús es amarillo. |
| The van is brown. | La camioneta es marrón. |
| The house is brown. | La casa es marrón. |
| The car is brown. | El coche es marrón. |
| The building is brown. | El edificio es marrón. |

## Mile Eight

| What is there? | ¿Qué hay? |
| There is... | Hay... |
| There's a motorcycle. | Hay una motocicleta. |
| There's a train. | Hay un tren. |
| There's a forest. | Hay un bosque. |
| There's a bike. | Hay una bicicleta. |
| There's a city. | Hay una ciudad. |
| There's a man. | Hay un hombre. |
| There's a woman. | Hay una mujer. |
| There's a mountain. | Hay una montaña. |

## Mile Nine

| My car is big. | Mi coche es grande. |
| My car is small. | Mi coche es pequeño. |
| My car is new. | Mi coche es nuevo. |
| My car is old. | Mi coche es viejo. |
| My car is beautiful. | Mi coche es lindo. |
| My car is ugly. | Mi coche es feo. |
| My car is expensive. | Mi coche es caro. |
| My car is inexpensive. | Mi coche es barato. |
| My car is fast. | Mi coche es rápido. |
| My car is slow. | Mi coche es lento. |

| My bike is big. | Mi bicicleta es grande. |
| My bike is small. | Mi bicicleta es pequeña. |
| My bike is new. | Mi bicicleta es nueva. |
| My bike is old. | Mi bicicleta es vieja. |
| My bike is beautiful. | Mi bicicleta es linda. |
| My bike is ugly. | Mi bicicleta es fea. |
| My bike is expensive. | Mi biciclea es cara. |
| My bike is inexpensive. | Mi bicicleta es barata. |

| | |
|---|---|
| My bike is fast. | Mi bicicleta es rápida. |
| My bike is slow. | Mi bicicleta es lenta. |

## Mile Ten

| | |
|---|---|
| Where are you going? | ¿A dónde vas? |
| I'm going to work. | Yo voy al trabajo. |
| I'm going to the city. | Yo voy a la ciudad. |
| I'm going to the office. | Yo voy a la oficina. |
| I'm going to the store. | Yo voy al almacén. |
| I'm going to the bank. | Yo voy al banco. |
| I'm going to the airport. | Yo voy al aeropuerto. |
| I'm going to school. | Yo voy a la escuela. |
| I'm going home. | Yo voy a casa. |

# LESSON 1

SALUDOS Y PRESENTACIONES

Greetings and Introductions

| Julio: | Buenos días. Mi nombre es Julio Martínez Valle. |
| Marta: | Mucho gusto. Soy Marta Moreno Vázquez. ¿Es usted de Colombia? |
| Julio: | No, soy de Venezuela. Usted es de España, ¿verdad? |
| Marta: | Sí. Hay muchos españoles en México. |

| Julio: | *Good morning. My name is Julio Martínez Valle.* |
| Marta: | *It's a pleasure to meet you. I'm Marta Moreno Vázquez. Are you from Colombia?* |
| Julio: | *No, I'm from Venezuela. You're from Spain, right?* |
| Marta: | *Yes. There are many Spaniards in Mexico.* |

# NEW VOCABULARY*

| | |
|---|---|
| América Latina | *Latin America* |
| Buenas noches. | *Good evening.* |
| Buenas tardes. | *Good afternoon.* |
| Buenos días. | *Good morning.* |
| el día | *day* |
| los Estados Unidos | *The United States* |
| estar | *to be* |
| Hasta luego. | *See you later.* |
| Hasta mañana. | *See you tomorrow.* |
| Hay . . . | *There is . . ./There are . . .* |
| ¡Hola! | *Hello!* |
| el hombre | *man* |
| latinoamericano/a | *Latin American (m/f)* |
| mi | *my* |
| Mucho gusto. | *Pleased to meet you.* |
| la mujer | *woman* |
| no | *no* |
| la noche | *night* |
| el nombre | *name* |
| señor | *Mr.; sir* |
| señora | *Mrs., Ms.; madam* |
| ser | *to be* |
| ser de | *to be from* |
| sí | *yes* |
| Soy . . . | *I am . . .* |
| su | *your* |
| ¿Verdad? | *Isn't that so?* |

* The abbreviations used in the new vocabulary lists are: *m* for "masculine," *f* for "feminine," *sg* for "singular," *pl* for "plural," *adv* for "adverb," *infml* for "informal," and *fml* for "formal."

# LESSON 2
## INFORMACIÓN
### Asking for Information

| | |
|---|---|
| Señorita Falcón: | Permiso, señor. Necesito información. |
| Señor Carrasco: | ¿En qué puedo servirle? |
| Señorita Falcón: | ¿Dónde está el hotel Fénix? |
| Señor Carrasco: | La dirección es Calle Once, número ocho dos uno. |
| Señorita Falcón: | Muchas gracias, señor. |

| | |
|---|---|
| Miss Falcón: | Excuse me, sir. I need some information. |
| Mr. Carrasco: | How can I help you? |
| Miss Falcón: | Where is the Phoenix Hotel? |
| Mr. Carrasco: | The address is 821 Eleventh Street. |
| Miss Falcón: | Thank you very much, sir. |

# NEW VOCABULARY

| | |
|---|---|
| al | *to the, at the* |
| la calle | *street* |
| cero | *zero* |
| cinco | *five* |
| ¿Cómo? | *What?; How?* |
| ¿Cómo es ella? | *What is she like?* |
| ¿Cómo está usted? | *How are you?* |
| ¿Comprende? | *Do you understand?* |
| ¿Cuál? | *What?; Which?* |
| ¿Cuál es su nombre? | *What is your name?* |
| cuatro | *four* |
| De nada. | *You're welcome.* |
| del | *from the, of the* |
| diez | *ten* |
| la dirección | *address* |
| ¿Dónde? | *Where?* |
| ¿Dónde está el centro? | *Where is downtown?* |
| dos | *two* |
| él | *he* |
| ella | *she* |
| ellas | *they (f)* |
| ellos | *they (m)* |
| ¿En qué puedo servirle? | *How can I help you?* |
| Estoy bien. | *I'm fine.* |
| Estoy perdido. | *I'm lost.* |
| Gracias. | *Thank you.* |
| el hotel | *hotel* |
| la información | *information* |
| Muchas gracias. | *Thank you very much.* |
| necesitar | *to need* |
| nosotras | *we (f)* |
| nosotros | *we (m)* |
| nueve | *nine* |
| números | *numbers* |
| ocho | *eight* |
| Permiso. | *Excuse me.* |

| | |
|---|---|
| ¿Puede ayudarme? | *Can you help me?* |
| ¿Qué? | *What?* |
| seis | *six* |
| siete | *seven* |
| tres | *three* |
| tú | *you (infml)* |
| Ud. | *you (fml)(from usted)* |
| Uds. | *you (pl)(from ustedes)* |
| uno | *one* |
| yo | *I* |

# LESSON 3
## LA HORA
### Clock Time

| Gabriel: | Buenos días, Anita. Soy yo, Gabriel. ¿Cuándo es la obra de teatro esta noche? |
| Anita: | Es a las nueve de la noche. ¿Qué hora es ahora? |
| Gabriel: | En mi reloj, son las nueve menos veinte. |
| Anita: | De acuerdo. ¡Hasta luego! |

| Gabriel: | *Hello, Anita. It's me, Gabriel. When is the play tonight?* |
| Anita: | *It's at nine o'clock in the evening. What time is it now?* |
| Gabriel: | *According to my watch, it's twenty to nine.* |
| Anita: | *Okay. See you later!* |

# NEW VOCABULARY

| | |
|---|---|
| A las seis en punto. | *At six o'clock sharp.* |
| ¿A qué hora? | *At what time?* |
| el animal | *animal* |
| anoche | *last night* |
| ¿Cuándo es? | *When is it?* |
| De acuerdo. | *Okay.* |
| de la mañana | *in the morning* |
| de la noche | *in the evening* |
| de la tarde | *in the afternoon* |
| Es a las nueve. | *It's at nine o'clock.* |
| Es la una. | *It's one o'clock.* |
| Es tarde. | *It's late.* |
| Es temprano. | *It's early.* |
| esta noche | *tonight* |
| Hasta luego. | *See you later.* |
| importante | *important* |
| la invitación | *invitation* |
| obra de teatro | *play* |
| ¿Qué hora es? | *What time is it?* |
| el reloj | *watch* |
| Son las nueve menos veinte. | *It's twenty to nine.* |
| Son las ocho. | *It's eight o'clock.* |
| Soy yo. | *It's me.* |

# LESSON 4
## EL TRABAJO
### Work

| | |
|---|---|
| Isabel: | Trabajo el lunes, martes y miércoles en la oficina y el jueves y viernes en la fábrica. |
| Andrés: | ¿Quién es su jefe? |
| Isabel: | El señor González. Es muy simpático. |
| Andrés: | ¿Y cuánto gana usted por año? |
| Isabel: | Gano el salario máximo. |
| Andrés: | ¡Qué bueno! |

| | |
|---|---|
| Isabel: | *On Mondays, Tuesdays and Wednesdays I work in the office and on Thursdays and Fridays I work in the factory.* |
| Andrés: | *Who is your boss?* |
| Isabel: | *Mr. Gonzalez. He is very nice.* |
| Andrés: | *And how much do you earn per year?* |
| Isabel: | *I earn the maximum salary.* |
| Andrés: | *Great!* |

# NEW VOCABULARY

| | |
|---|---|
| antipático/a | unfriendly (m/f) |
| buscar | to search |
| buscar un trabajo | to look for a job |
| ¿Cuánto ganas? | How much do you earn? |
| el dependiente | clerk |
| descansar | to rest |
| desempleado/a | unemployed (m/f) |
| los días laborables | work days |
| el dinero | money |
| domingo | Sunday |
| el/la ejecutivo/a | executive (m/f) |
| empleado/a | employed (m/f) |
| escuchar | to listen |
| la fábrica | factory |
| el fin de semana | weekend |
| el/la fotógrafo | photographer (m/f) |
| ganar | to earn |
| hablar | to talk |
| el jefe/la jefa | boss (m/f) |
| jueves | Thursday |
| lunes | Monday |
| el maestro | teacher |
| martes | Tuesday |
| miércoles | Wednesday |
| la oficina | office |
| por hora | hourly |
| por mes | monthly |
| por semana | weekly |
| ¡Qué bueno! | How wonderful! |
| ¿Quién? | Who? |
| sábado | Saturday |
| el salario | salary |
| simpático/a | nice (m/f) |
| el taxista | taxi driver |
| trabajar | to work |
| el trabajo | job |
| el/la vice presidente/a | vice president (m/f) |
| viernes | Friday |

# LESSON 5
## EL TIEMPO, LOS MESES, LAS ESTACIONES
### Weather, Months, Seasons

Elena:     Hace mucho calor en el verano. ¿Cuántos grados hace hoy?
Jesús:     Treinta y dos grados centígrados, por lo menos.
Elena:     ¿Cómo es el tiempo aquí en primavera?
Jesús:     En esta estación del año, el tiempo es menos caliente y menos húmedo.

Elena:     It's very hot in the summer. What's the temperature today?
Jesús:     Thirty-two degrees centigrade, at least.
Elena:     What is the weather like here in spring?
Jesús:     In that season of the year, the weather is not as hot and it's less humid.

# NEW VOCABULARY

| | |
|---|---|
| aquel | *that* |
| aprender | *to learn* |
| beber | *to drink* |
| caliente | *hot* |
| centígrados | *centigrade* |
| comer | *to eat* |
| ¿Cuántos grados hace? | *How many degrees is it?* |
| en [el] otoño | *in autumn* |
| en [la] primavera | *in spring* |
| en [el] verano | *in summer* |
| ese | *that* |
| la estación | *season* |
| este | *this* |
| los grados | *degrees* |
| Hace buen tiempo. | *It's nice out.* |
| Hace calor. | *It's warm.* |
| Hace fresco. | *It's cool.* |
| Hace frío. | *It's cold.* |
| Hace húmedo. | *It's humid.* |
| el invierno | *winter* |
| leer | *to read* |
| Llueve. | *It's raining.* |
| por lo menos | *at least* |
| el tiempo | *weather* |
| ¿Qué tiempo hace? | *What's the weather like?* |

# LESSON 6
## ROPA, COLORES, TALLAS
### Clothing, Colors, Sizes

| | |
|---|---|
| Florinda: | Voy de compras. La tienda abre a las diez menos cuarto. |
| Antonio: | Vamos juntos. Necesito un traje de verano. |
| Florinda: | Deseo un vestido de seda verde. |
| Antonio: | Muy bien. |

| | |
|---|---|
| Florinda: | *I'm going shopping. The store opens at nine forty-five.* |
| Antonio: | *Let's go together. I need a summer suit.* |
| Florinda: | *I want a green silk dress.* |
| Antonio: | *Okay.* |

# NEW VOCABULARY

| | |
|---|---|
| abrir | *to open* |
| el algodón | *cotton* |
| amarillo/a | *yellow (m/f)* |
| azul | *blue* |
| blanco/a | *white (m/f)* |
| la blusa | *blouse* |
| la camisa | *shirt* |
| el color | *color* |
| escribir | *to write* |
| extra-grande | *extra-large* |
| grande | *large* |
| ir | *to go* |
| ir de compras | *to go shopping* |
| la lana | *wool* |
| mediano/a | *medium (m/f)* |
| necesitar | *to need* |
| negro/a | *black (m/f)* |
| los pantalones | *pants* |
| partir | *to leave* |
| pequeño/a | *small (m/f)* |
| ¿Qué talla lleva Ud.? | *What size do you wear?* |
| la ropa nueva | *new clothing* |
| la seda | *silk* |
| la talla | *size* |
| el tamaño | *size* |
| la tela | *material* |
| la tienda | *store* |
| el traje | *suit* |
| Vamos juntos. | *Let's go together.* |
| verde | *green* |
| el vestido | *dress* |
| vivir | *to live* |
| los zapatos | *shoes* |

# LESSON 7
## EL CUERPO Y LA SALUD
### The Body and Health

Julián:  ¿Estás lista, Marisa?
Marisa:  No tengo ganas de correr. Tengo dolores en todo el cuerpo: la espalda, las manos . . .
Julián:  ¿Estás enferma?
Marisa:  No creo.
Julián:  Tienes que descansar.
Marisa:  Tienes razón.


Julián:  *Are you ready, Marisa?*
Marisa:  *I don't feel like running. I've got pain in my whole body: my back, my arms . . .*
Julián:  *Are you sick?*
Marisa:  *I don't think so.*
Julián:  *You have to rest.*
Marisa:  *You're right.*

# NEW VOCABULARY

| | |
|---|---|
| agudo/a | *sharp (m/f)* |
| constante | *constant* |
| correr | *to run* |
| creer | *to believe; to think* |
| el cuerpo | *body* |
| descansar | *to rest* |
| el dolor | *pain* |
| enfermo/a | *sick (m/f)* |
| la espalda | *back* |
| hacer | *to do, to make* |
| hacer ejercicio | *to exercise* |
| hacer un viaje | *to take a trip* |
| hormigueo | *tingling* |
| levantar pesas | *to lift weights* |
| ligero/a | *slight (m/f)* |
| listo/a | *ready (m/f)* |
| las manos | *hands* |
| montar en bicicleta | *to ride a bicycle* |
| nadar | *to swim* |
| no tener razón | *to be wrong* |
| quemante | *burning* |
| tener | *to have* |
| tener calor | *to be warm* |
| tener cuidado | *to be careful* |
| tener dolor de | *to feel a pain (in)* |
| tener frío | *to be cold* |
| tener ganas de | *to feel like* |
| tener hambre | *to be hungry* |
| tener que | *to have to* |
| tener razón | *to be right* |
| tener sed | *to be thirsty* |
| tener veinticinco años | *to be twenty-five years old* |

# LESSON 8
## RELACIONES FAMILIARES
### Family Relationships

José:   Tu prima Carmen acepta nuestra invitación a la boda.

Marta:  Toda nuestra familia va a estar reunida para la boda.

José:   ¡Qué maravilla! Hace mucho tiempo que no estamos juntos.


José:   *Your cousin Carmen accepted our wedding invitation.*

Marta:  *All our family will be together at the ceremony.*

José:   *How wonderful! It's been a long time since we we've been together.*

# NEW VOCABULARY

| | |
|---|---|
| la abuela | *grandmother* |
| el abuelo | *grandfather* |
| aceptar | *to accept* |
| la boda | *wedding* |
| encontrar | *to meet* |
| estar reunidos | *to be together* |
| la familia | *family* |
| Hace mucho tiempo. | *It's been a long time./A long time ago . . .* |
| la hermana | *sister* |
| el hermano | *brother* |
| la invitación | *invitation* |
| la madre | *mother* |
| mi | *my* |
| mis | *my (pl)* |
| nuestra | *our (f)* |
| nuestras | *our (f pl)* |
| nuestro | *our (m)* |
| nuestros | *our (pl)* |
| el padre | *father* |
| los parientes | *relatives* |
| la prima | *female cousin* |
| el primo | *male cousin* |
| ¡Qué maravilla! | *How wonderful!* |
| su | *his, her, your, their* |
| sus | *his, her, your, their* |
| la tía | *aunt* |
| el tío | *uncle* |
| tu | *your* |
| tus | *your (pl)* |
| visitar | *to visit* |

# LESSON 9
## COMIDA
### Food

| | |
|---|---|
| Elvira: | Vamos a comprar carne. |
| Aurelio: | Tenemos que comprar verduras y frutas también. |
| Elvira: | ¿Cuáles deseas? |
| Aurelio: | Una caja de fresas, una bolsa de manzanas y esa piña. |

| | |
|---|---|
| Elvira: | *We are going to buy meat.* |
| Aurelio: | *We also have to buy vegetables and fruit.* |
| Elvira: | *Which do you want?* |
| Aurelio: | *A box of strawberries, a bag of apples, and that pineapple.* |

# NEW VOCABULARY

| | |
|---|---|
| a | to, at |
| el bistec | steak |
| la bolsa | bag |
| la caja | box |
| la carne | meat |
| con | with |
| conmigo | with me |
| contigo | with you |
| ¿Cuál? | Which?/Which one? |
| de | of, from |
| él | him |
| ella | her |
| ellas | they (f) |
| ellos | they (m) |
| en | in, on |
| la ensalada | salad |
| el envase de leche | container of milk |
| la fresa | strawberry |
| la fruta | fruit |
| hacer compras | to go shopping |
| el kilo | kilogram |
| la | her, you, it |
| los lácteos | milk products |
| las | you, them (f) |
| la lechuga | lettuce |
| la libra | pound |
| el litro | liter |
| lo | him, you, it |
| los | you, them |
| la manzana | apple |
| me | me |
| mí | me |
| nos | us |
| la onza | ounce |
| el pan | bread |
| los panecillos | rolls |

| | |
|---|---|
| para | for |
| el peso | weight |
| por | for |
| el queso | cheese |
| la salchicha | sausage |
| el supermercado | supermarket |
| te | you |
| ti | you |
| los tomates | tomatoes |
| las uvas | grapes |
| venir | to come |
| las verduras | vegetables |

# LESSON 10
## GUSTOS
### Likes and Dislikes

| | |
|---|---|
| Señora Martinez: | Deseo comprar algo especial para mi sobrino. |
| Vendedor: | Hay muchos aparatos muy buenos aquí. A los jóvenes les gustan los aparatos de discos compactos. |
| Señora Martinez: | Tal vez le daría un aparato de discos compactos. |

| | |
|---|---|
| Mrs. Martinez: | I want to buy something special for my nephew. |
| Salesman: | There are many very good appliances here. Young people like compact disc players. |
| Mrs. Martinez: | Perhaps I'll buy him a compact disc player. |

# NEW VOCABULARY

| | |
|---|---|
| algo | *something* |
| el aparato de discos compactos | *compact disc player* |
| los aparatos | *appliances* |
| la aspiradora | *vacuum cleaner* |
| dar | *to give* |
| dar un regalo | *to give a gift* |
| de confianza | *reliable* |
| decir | *to say, to tell* |
| demasiado barato/a | *too cheap (m/f)* |
| demasiado caro/a | *too expensive (m/f)* |
| desear | *to want, to wish* |
| el disco compacto | *compact disc, CD* |
| los electrodomésticos | *kitchen appliances* |
| faltar | *to be lacking* |
| gustar | *to like* |
| el horno | *oven* |
| la lavadora | *washing machine* |
| el lavaplatos | *dishwasher* |
| le | *to him, to her, to you* |
| les | *to them, to you* |
| la marca | *brand* |
| me | *to me* |
| el microondas | *microwave* |
| nos | *to us* |
| parecer | *to seem* |
| razonable | *reasonable* |
| el refrigerador | *refrigerator* |
| la secadora | *dryer* |
| el sobrino | *nephew* |
| tal vez | *perhaps; maybe* |
| te | *to you* |

# LESSON 11
## COMIENDO EN LOS RESTAURANTES
### Eating at Restaurants

| | |
|---|---|
| Juan Carlos: | ¿Puedo ver el menú? ¿Cuál es la sopa del día? |
| Mesera: | La sopa del día es puré de maíz. |
| Juan Carlos: | Todo huele muy bien. ¿Se puede fumar aquí? |
| Mesera: | Esta sección es de no fumar. |

| | |
|---|---|
| Juan Carlos: | Can I see the menu? What is the soup of the day? |
| Waitress: | The soup of the day is corn soup. |
| Juan Carlos: | Everything smells delicious! Is smoking permitted here? |
| Waitress: | This is a no smoking section. |

# NEW VOCABULARY

| | |
|---|---|
| almorzar | to eat lunch |
| el aperitivo | aperitif |
| comer bien | to eat well |
| la cuchara | spoon |
| el cuchillo | knife |
| dormir | to sleep |
| encontrar | to meet |
| la especialidad de la casa | house specialty |
| fumar | to smoke |
| el menú | menu |
| mostrar | to show |
| oler | to smell |
| los platos típicos | typical dishes |
| poder | to be able |
| el postre | dessert |
| la propina | tip |
| el puré de maíz | corn soup |
| el restaurante | restaurant |
| se | one (pronoun), you (infml) |
| ¿Se puede fumar aquí? | Can you smoke here? |
| la sección | section |
| la sopa del día | daily soup |
| el tenedor | fork |
| tomar el almuerzo | to eat lunch |
| tomar la cena | to eat dinner |
| tomar el desayuno | to eat breakfast |
| ver | to see |
| volver | to return |

# LESSON 12
## POR TELÉFONO
### Making a Phone Call

| | |
|---|---|
| Javier: | Quiero hacer una llamada internacional, persona a persona. |
| Operadora: | ¿Con quién quiere usted hablar? |
| Javier: | Quiero hablar con mi esposa. |
| Operadora: | Lo siento. La línea internacional está ocupada. |

| | |
|---|---|
| *Javier:* | *I want to make an international, person to person call.* |
| *Operator:* | *With whom do you want to speak?* |
| *Javier:* | *I want to speak with my wife.* |
| *Operator:* | *I'm sorry. The international line is busy.* |

# NEW VOCABULARY

| | |
|---|---|
| a menudo | *often* |
| ¿A quién? | *To whom?* |
| allí | *there* |
| aquí | *here* |
| ayer | *yesterday* |
| cargar | *to charge* |
| ¿Con quién? | *With whom?* |
| ¿De quién? | *Whose?* |
| entender | *to understand* |
| el esposo | *husband* |
| estar ocupado | *to be busy* |
| la guía telefónica | *telephone book* |
| hoy | *today* |
| la línea | *line* |
| la llamada | *call* |
| la llamada de larga distancia | *long-distance call* |
| la llamada internacional | *international call* |
| la llamada local | *local call* |
| la llamada a cobro revertido | *collect call* |
| llamar | *to call* |
| Lo siento. | *I'm sorry.* |
| mañana | *tomorrow* |
| marcar un número | *to dial a number* |
| el número equivocado | *wrong number* |
| obtener información | *to get information* |
| el/la operador/a | *operator* |
| ¿Para quién? | *For whom?* |
| pensar | *to think* |
| perder | *to lose* |
| persona a persona | *person to person* |
| querer | *to wish; to want* |
| quién | *who, whom* |
| sentir | *to feel; to regret* |
| el servicio telefónico | *telephone service* |
| siempre | *always* |

# LESSON 13
## EN LA JOYERÍA
### At the Jewelry Store

Vendedora: ¿En qué puedo servirle?

Germán: Vengo a comprarle una pulsera a mi esposa. No sé nada de joyas pero conozco bien a mi esposa. A ella le gustan las joyas simples.

Vendedora: Tenemos una venta especial esta semana.

Germán: ¡Qué bueno!

Saleswoman: *How can I help you?*

Germán: *I've come to buy a bracelet for my wife. I don't know anything about jewelry but I know my wife well. She likes simple jewelry.*

Saleswoman: *We have a special sale this week.*

Germán: *How wonderful!*

# NEW VOCABULARY

| | |
|---|---|
| el anillo | ring |
| el aniversario de la boda | wedding anniversary |
| los aretes | earrings |
| el collar | necklace |
| conocer | to be acquainted with |
| el cumpleaños | birthday |
| los diamantes | diamonds |
| ¿En qué puedo servirle? | How can I help you? |
| especial | special |
| la joyería | jewelry store |
| el oro | gold |
| merecer | to deserve |
| ofrecer | to offer |
| pagar con una tarjeta de crédito | to pay with a credit card |
| pedir | to ask for |
| la plata | silver |
| producir | to produce |
| la pulsera | bracelet |
| el recibo | receipt |
| el reloj | watch |
| repetir | to repeat |
| el rubí | ruby |
| saber | to know |
| servir | to serve |
| simple | simple |
| venir | to come |
| la venta | sale |

# LESSON 14
## EN LA FARMACÍA
### At the Pharmacy

Guadalupe:          Tengo una receta del médico. La
                    necesito lo más pronto posible.
Farmacéutico:       Se la lleno en quince minutos.
Guadalupe:          ¿Qué recomienda para un resfriado?
Farmacéutico:       Puede escoger entre muchas marcas
                    de jarabe para la tos o pastillas para
                    la tos.


Guadalupe:          *I have a doctor's prescription. I need it
                    as soon as possible.*
Pharmacist:         *I'll fill it for you in fifteen minutes.*
Guadalupe:          *What do you recommend for a cold?*
Pharmacist:         *You can select from among many
                    brands of cough syrups or cough drops.*

# NEW VOCABULARY

| | |
|---|---|
| el antiácido | antacid |
| la aspirina | aspirin |
| los cosméticos | cosmetics |
| el desodorante | deodorant |
| dirigir | to drive, to lead |
| las drogas | drugs |
| los escalofríos | chills |
| escoger | to choose |
| el farmacéutico | pharmacist |
| la farmacia | pharmacy |
| el jarabe para la tos | cough syrup |
| llenar una receta | to fill a prescription |
| las pastillas para la tos | cough drops |
| proteger | to protect |
| la receta | prescription |
| recetar un remedio | to prescribe a medicine |
| recomendar | to recommend |
| el resfriado | cold |
| salir | to leave |
| la vitamina | vitamin |

# LESSON 15
## ACTIVIDADES DIARIAS
### Daily Activities

| | |
|---|---|
| Julio: | Me levanto ahora y me baño. |
| Antonia: | ¿Por qué a esta hora tan temprana de la mañana? |
| Julio: | Comienza hoy el nuevo horario de trabajo. Voy a reunirme con el nuevo jefe a las siete y media. |
| Antonia: | ¡No lo puedo creer! No te vas a acostumbrar a trabajar estas largas horas. Vas a enfermarte. |

| | |
|---|---|
| *Julio:* | *I'm getting up now and I'm taking a bath.* |
| *Antonia:* | *Why at this early hour of the morning?* |
| *Julio:* | *The new work schedule begins today. I'm going to meet the new boss at seven-thirty.* |
| *Antonia:* | *I can't believe it! You won't get used to working such long hours. You'll get sick.* |

# NEW VOCABULARY

| | |
|---|---|
| acostarse | *to go to bed* |
| acostumbrarse | *to get accustomed* |
| bañarse | *to bathe* |
| cepillarse | *to brush one's teeth* |
| comenzar | *to begin* |
| ¿Cómo se llama Ud.? | *What's your name?* |
| creer | *to believe* |
| desayunar | *to have breakfast* |
| enfermarse | *to get ill* |
| el horario de trabajo | *work schedule* |
| irse a trabajar | *to go to work* |
| lavarse | *to wash oneself* |
| levantarse | *to get up* |
| llamarse | *to be called, to be named* |
| me | *myself* |
| muy temprano | *very early* |
| nos | *ourselves, one another* |
| peinarse | *to comb one's hair* |
| poner | *to put, to place* |
| ponerse la ropa | *to put on clothes* |
| por la mañana | *in the morning, a.m.* |
| quitarse la ropa | *to take off clothes* |
| reunirse | *to get together* |
| se | *himself, herself, yourself, themselves, yourselves, each other* |
| secarse | *to dry oneself* |
| te | *yourself (infml)* |
| tomar un baño | *to take a bath* |
| vestirse | *to get dressed* |

# LESSON 16
## EN EL AUTOBÚS
### Traveling by Bus

| | |
|---|---|
| Rubén: | Acabo de llegar a la estación de autobuses. ¿Qué número tomo para llegar a tu casa? |
| Amiga: | Es mejor tomar el número ocho. El número once es más lento que el ocho. |
| Rubén: | ¿Dónde bajo? |
| Amiga: | Bajas en el cine Oro. Al bajar, sigues derecho. |

| | |
|---|---|
| *Rubén:* | *I've just arrived at the bus station. What bus do I take to your house?* |
| *Friend:* | *It's better to take number eight. Number eleven is slower than number eight.* |
| *Rubén:* | *Where do I get off?* |
| *Friend:* | *You get off at the Oro Theater. After getting off, you walk straight ahead.* |

# NEW VOCABULARY

| | |
|---|---|
| a la derecha | *to the right* |
| a la izquierda | *to the left* |
| al bajar | *upon getting off* |
| acabar de | *to have just* |
| la avenida | *avenue* |
| bajar del autobús | *to get off the bus* |
| coger el autobús | *to take the bus* |
| la cuadra | *street block* |
| distinguir | *to distinguish* |
| en dirección de | *in the direction of* |
| la estación de autobuses | *bus station* |
| más | *more* |
| más lento que | *slower than* |
| mayor | *bigger, older* |
| mejor | *better* |
| menor | *smaller, younger* |
| menos | *less* |
| menos interesante que | *less interesting than* |
| la parada | *bus stop* |
| el pasaje | *ticket* |
| el pasajero | *passenger* |
| peor | *worse* |
| la plaza | *plaza* |
| rumbo a | *bound for* |
| seguir | *to follow* |
| seguir derecho | *to go straight ahead* |
| subir al autobús | *to get on the bus* |
| tan importante como | *as important as* |
| tanto | *as much, as many* |
| tomar el autobús | *to take the bus* |

# LESSON 17
## EN EL TREN
## Traveling by Train

Pepe:      Dígame, señorita, ¿a qué hora parte el tren para Santiago?

Agente:     Hay asientos para la partida de las dos y media de la mañana.

Pepe:      ¿Cuánto es un pasaje de ida y vuelta de primera clase?

Agente:     Ochenta y cinco euros.

Pepe:      Deme dos pasajes de segunda. ¿Puedo traer este baúl conmigo a bordo?

Agente:     No, señor. Llévelo al maletero.

Pepe:      *Tell me, miss, at what time does the train for Santiago leave?*

Agent:      *There are seats for the two-thirty a.m. departure.*

Pepe:      *How much is a first-class round-trip ticket?*

Agent:      *Eighty-five euros.*

Pepe:      *Give me two second-class tickets. Can I bring this trunk on board with me?*

Agent:      *No, sir. Take it to the porter.*

# NEW VOCABULARY

| | |
|---|---|
| a bordo | *on board* |
| el baúl | *trunk* |
| caer | *to fall* |
| coche-cama | *sleeping car* |
| coche-comedor | *dining car* |
| el conductor | *conductor* |
| el cual | *which* |
| ¡Deme dos! | *Give me two!* |
| ¡Dígame! | *Tell me!* |
| el equipaje | *baggage* |
| expreso | *express* |
| hacer las maletas | *to pack bags* |
| llegadas y partidas | *arrivals and departures* |
| ¡Llévelo! | *Take it!* |
| local | *local* |
| el maletero | *porter* |
| la partida | *departure* |
| el pasaje de ida y vuelta | *round-trip ticket* |
| los pasajes de segunda clase | *second-class tickets* |
| primera clase | *first class* |
| que | *who, whom, which, that* |
| reservar un asiento | *to reserve a seat* |
| traer | *to bring* |
| el transbordo | *transfer* |
| el vagón | *train car* |

# LESSON 18
## ALQUILANDO UN COCHE
### Renting a Car

| | |
|---|---|
| Vicente: | El coche más pequeño y más barato para alquilar por semana es este Ford. |
| Inés: | ¡Es carísimo! |
| Vicente: | No tenemos ningún coche más económico. Es la mejor oferta de la agencia. |
| Inés: | ¿Dónde firmo el contrato de arrendamiento? |

| | |
|---|---|
| Vicente: | The smallest and cheapest car to rent weekly is this Ford. |
| Inés: | It's very expensive! |
| Vicente: | We don't have any cheaper cars. It's the agency's best offer. |
| Inés: | Where do I sign the leasing contract? |

# NEW VOCABULARY

| | |
|---|---|
| algo | something |
| alguien | somebody |
| algún | some |
| alquilar un coche | to rent a car |
| auxilio de carretera | road service |
| carísimo/a | very expensive (m/f) |
| el coche | car |
| el coche de alquiler | rental car |
| el coche más pequeño | the smallest car |
| construir | to build |
| destruir | to destroy |
| devolver el coche | to return the car |
| firmar el contrato de arrendamiento | to sign the leasing contract |
| incluir | to include |
| instruir | to instruct |
| el internet | the Web, Internet |
| los kilómetros | kilometers |
| la licencia de conducir | driver's license |
| llenar el depósito | to fill the tank |
| millas sin límite | unlimited mileage |
| nada | nothing |
| nadie | nobody |
| ni . . . ni | neither . . . nor |
| ni este coche ni aquel coche | neither this car nor that car |
| ningún | none |
| ningún coche | no car |
| nunca | never |
| o . . . o | either . . . or |
| o este coche o aquel coche | either this car or that car |
| obtener seguros | to obtain insurance |
| la oferta | offer |
| pagar por milla | to pay by the mile |
| reírse | to laugh |
| siempre | always |
| también | also |
| tampoco | neither |

# LESSON 19
## EN LA GASOLINERA
### At the Gas Station

| | |
|---|---|
| José: | Por favor, revise la batería. El motor se paró de repente. |
| Manuela: | A la batería le falta agua. |
| José: | ¡No es posible! La compré la semana pasada. No sé qué pasó. |

| | |
|---|---|
| *José:* | *Please, check the battery. The motor stopped suddenly.* |
| *Manuela:* | *The battery needs water.* |
| *José:* | *That is impossible! I bought it last week. I don't know what happened.* |

# NEW VOCABULARY

| | |
|---|---|
| el año pasado | *last year* |
| arrancar | *to turn on the car* |
| el arranque | *ignition* |
| ayer | *yesterday* |
| el chequeo | *check-up* |
| de repente | *suddenly* |
| el embrague | *clutch* |
| los frenos | *brakes* |
| la gasolinera | *gas station* |
| inflar las llantas | *to inflate the tires* |
| Le falta agua a la batería. | *The battery needs water.* |
| el mecánico | *mechanic* |
| el motor | *motor* |
| no es posible | *it isn't possible* |
| el parabrisas | *windshield* |
| pararse | *to stop* |
| poner aceite | *to put in oil* |
| revisar la batería | *to check the battery* |
| la semana pasada | *last week* |
| el taller | *repair shop* |

# LESSON 20
## ALQUILANDO UN APARTAMENTO
### Renting an Apartment

| | |
|---|---|
| Anita: | ¿Qué tipo de apartamento busca usted ahora? |
| Ricardo: | Debe tener varios dormitorios y baños. |
| Anita: | ¿Ya buscó tal apartamento? |
| Ricardo: | Los alquileres son altísimos. |
| Anita: | ¿Cuánto paga usted por su apartamento actual? |
| Ricardo: | Pago ochocientos por mes. |

| | |
|---|---|
| Anita: | *What type of apartment are you looking for at this time?* |
| Ricardo: | *It must have several bedrooms and bathrooms.* |
| Anita: | *Have you already looked for such an apartment?* |
| Ricardo: | *The rents are very high.* |
| Anita: | *How much are you paying for your present apartment?* |
| Ricardo: | *I pay eight hundred per month.* |

# NEW VOCABULARY

| | |
|---|---|
| el agente de inmuebles | real estate broker |
| el apartamento sin muebles | unfurnished apartment |
| el baño | bathroom |
| buscar un apartamento | to look for an apartment |
| la calefacción | heating |
| comenzar | to begin |
| continuar | to continue |
| el cuarto amueblado | furnished room |
| el dormitorio | bedroom |
| e | and (before "i") |
| la electricidad | electricity |
| empezar | to begin |
| entregar | to deliver |
| enviar | to send |
| evaluar | to evaluate |
| el gas | gas |
| indicar | to indicate |
| leer los clasificados | to read the classified ads |
| pagar un alquiler altísimo | to pay a very high price |
| pagar una cuota de seguridad | to pay a security deposit |
| pegar | to hit |
| preferir un barrio | to prefer a neighborhood |
| la terraza | terrace |
| tocar | to touch |
| tocarle a uno | to be one's turn |
| u | or (before "o") |
| variar | to vary |

# LESSON 21
## EN EL CONSULTORIO MÉDICO
### At the Doctor's Office

| Señor Atlas: | Cuando me levanté esta mañana estuve enfermo. Tuve fuertes dolores de cabeza y de estómago. Tomé dos aspirinas. |
| Doctora: | ¿Continúan los dolores? |
| Señor Atlas: | Poco a poco comenzaron a disminuir. |
| Doctora: | Usted comió demasiado anoche. |

| Mr. Atlas: | *When I got up this morning I was sick. I had a bad headache and a stomachache. I took two aspirins.* |
| Doctor: | *Is the pain continuing?* |
| Mr. Atlas: | *Little by little it is beginning to diminish.* |
| Doctor: | *You ate too much last night.* |

# NEW VOCABULARY

| | |
|---|---|
| comer demasiado | *to eat too much* |
| el consultorio | *doctor's office* |
| descansar | *to rest* |
| disminuir | *to diminish* |
| estar enfermo | *to be sick* |
| la fiebre | *fever* |
| guardar cama | *to stay in bed* |
| los líquidos | *liquids* |
| los mareos | *dizziness* |
| las nauseas | *nausea* |
| poco a poco | *little by little* |
| tener dolor de cabeza | *to have a headache* |
| tomar dos aspirinas | *to take two aspirins* |
| tomar la temperatura | *to take a temperature* |
| tomar remedio | *to take a medicine* |
| tomar té | *to drink tea* |

# LESSON 22
## CON EL DENTISTA
### At the Dentist's

| | |
|---|---|
| Aurora: | Seguí sus consejos. Me cepillé tres veces al día y usé la seda dental. Pero anoche las encías se me pusieron rojas y se hincharon. |
| Dentista: | ¿Dónde le duele? Me parece que murió la raíz. |
| Aurora: | ¿Tiene que arrancarme la muela? |
| Dentista: | ¡Claro que no! |

| | |
|---|---|
| Aurora: | *I followed your advice. I brushed three times a day and I used dental floss. But last night my gums became red and they swelled up.* |
| Dentist: | *Where does it hurt? I think the root has died.* |
| Aurora: | *Do you have to pull my tooth?* |
| Dentist: | *Of course not!* |

# NEW VOCABULARY

| | |
|---|---|
| arrancar una muela | to pull out a tooth |
| la boca | mouth |
| la carie | cavity |
| cepillarse | to brush |
| el cepillo de dientes | toothbrush |
| ¡Claro que no! | Of course not! |
| el diente | tooth |
| dormir | to sleep |
| dolerle a uno | to hurt |
| el empaste | filling |
| examinar | to examine |
| hacerse | to become |
| hincharse | to swell |
| los labios | lips |
| la lengua | tongue |
| llegarse | to become |
| morir | to die |
| la pasta de dientes | toothpaste |
| la placa | plaque |
| ponerse nervioso | to become nervous |
| ponerse rojo | to become red |
| la raíz | root |
| el sarro | tartar |
| la seda dental | dental floss |
| seguir consejos | to follow advice |
| volverse loco | to go crazy |

# LESSON 23
## COMPRANDO UNA COMPUTADORA
### Buying a Computer

Oscar: ¿Cómo estás, Rafaela? ¿Qué llevas ahí?

Rafaela: Conduje a Computer World y compré una computadora. Quiero usar el correo electrónico.

Oscar: Para usar el correo electrónico, necesitas tener un proveedor de servicio al internet.

Rafaela: Eso ya lo sé. Hazme un favor, Oscar. Ayúdame a instalar la computadora.

Oscar: ¡Por supuesto!


Oscar: How are you, Rafaela? What do you have there?

Rafaela: I drove to Computer World and I bought a computer. I want to use e-mail.

Oscar: To use e-mail, you need to have an Internet service provider.

Rafaela: I know that. Do me a favor, Oscar. Help me install my computer.

Oscar: Of course!

# NEW VOCABULARY

| | |
|---|---|
| el archivo | *file* |
| ayudar | *to help* |
| la computadora | *computer* |
| conducir | *to drive* |
| conseguir | *to obtain* |
| el correo electrónico | *e-mail* |
| ¡Di! | *Say!* |
| los discos | *disks* |
| ¡Haz! | *Do!* |
| la impresora | *printer* |
| instalar | *to install* |
| el internet | *Internet* |
| láser | *laser* |
| el navegador | *navigator* |
| navegar en la red | *to surf the Web* |
| la página Web | *Web page* |
| la pantalla | *monitor* |
| ¡Pon! | *Put!* |
| los programas | *programs* |
| el proveedor de servicio | *service provider* |
| el ratón | *mouse* |
| ¡Sal! | *Leave!* |
| ¡Sé! | *Be!* |
| el teclado | *keyboard* |
| ¡Ten! | *Have!* |
| la tienda | *store* |
| traducir | *to translate* |
| traer | *to bring* |
| ¡Ve! | *Go!* |
| ¡Ven! | *Come!* |

# LESSON 24
## EN LA TAQUILLA DEL TEATRO
### At the Theater Box Office

| | |
|---|---|
| Virginia: | Deme dos butacas de platea para mañana. |
| Taquillero: | ¿Leyó usted que la producción comenzó a representarse en Madrid? Fue el mejor éxito de la temporada. |
| Virginia: | ¿A qué hora empieza? |
| Taquillero: | El telón va a subir a las ocho y habrá dos entreactos. |

| | |
|---|---|
| *Virginia:* | *Give me two orchestra seats for tomorrow.* |
| *Box office agent:* | *Did you read that the production began playing in Madrid? It was the biggest hit of the season.* |
| *Virginia:* | *At what time does it begin?* |
| *Box office agent:* | *The curtain goes up at eight and there will be two intermissions.* |

# NEW VOCABULARY

| | |
|---|---|
| abuchear | *to boo* |
| el actor | *actor* |
| la actriz | *actress* |
| la actuación | *acting* |
| aplaudir | *to applaud* |
| asistir a un estreno | *to attend a premiere* |
| las butacas de platea | *orchestra seats* |
| caer | *to fall* |
| comprar entradas | *to buy tickets* |
| creer | *to believe* |
| el crítico | *critic* |
| dar un premio | *to give a prize* |
| ¡Démelo! | *Give it to me!* |
| el entreacto | *intermission* |
| el éxito de la temporada | *season's hit* |
| la primera fila | *first row* |
| el/la protagonista | *lead actor/actress* |
| el público | *audience* |
| representar | *to perform* |
| la reseña | *review* |
| sentarse en la galería | *to seat in the balcony* |
| subir | *to go up* |
| la taquilla | *ticket booth* |
| el telón | *curtain* |

# LESSON 25
## ¡A REGATEAR!
### Bargaining

| | |
|---|---|
| Doña Florinda: | ¿Cuánto cuesta esa cómoda? |
| Don Vicente: | Llevaba un precio de tres mil euros. |
| Doña Florinda: | No vale tanto. |
| Don Vicente: | Se lo dejo en la mitad del precio original. |
| Doña Florinda: | ¡Menudo descuento! |

| | |
|---|---|
| *Doña Florinda:* | *How much is that chest of drawers?* |
| *Don Vicente:* | *It had a price tag of three thousand euros.* |
| *Doña Florinda:* | *It's not worth that much.* |
| *Don Vicente:* | *I'll sell it to you for half the original price.* |
| *Doña Florinda:* | *What a discount!* |

# NEW VOCABULARY

| | |
|---|---|
| la cómoda | chest of drawers |
| ¿Cuánto cuesta? | How much is it? |
| la cuenta | bill |
| de joven | as a youngster, when I was young |
| el descuento | discount |
| la etiqueta | label |
| llevar un precio | to have a price |
| el mercado de artículos usados | flea market |
| la mitad del precio | half price |
| No vale tanto. | It's not worth so/that much. |
| ofrecer un precio | to offer a price |
| pagar | to pay |
| el precio fijo | fixed price |
| regatear | to bargain |
| siempre | always |
| todo el año pasado | all last year |
| el último precio | final price |
| el vendedor | salesman |

# LESSON 26
## BUSCAR UN TRABAJO
### Looking for a Job

| | |
|---|---|
| Señor Navarro: | ¿Qué obligaciones tuvo en su trabajo? |
| Anita: | Organizaba una campaña de ventas de computadoras. |
| Señor Navarro: | Usted tuvo mucho éxito en la Celso. ¿Por qué dejó usted la posición? |
| Anita: | No hubo posibilidad de ascenso. Mi jefe era joven y altamente competente. |

| | |
|---|---|
| *Mr. Navarro:* | *What duties did you have at your job?* |
| *Anita:* | *I was organizing a computer sales campaign.* |
| *Mr. Navarro:* | *You had a great deal of success at Celso. Why did you leave the position?* |
| *Anita:* | *There was no opportunity for promotion. My boss was very young and highly qualified.* |

# NEW VOCABULARY

| | |
|---|---|
| altamente | *highly* |
| el anuncio de trabajo | *job announcement* |
| el ascenso | *promotion* |
| buscar un trabajo | *to look for a job* |
| la campaña de ventas | *sales campaign* |
| competente | *qualified; competent* |
| la computadora | *computer* |
| dejar una posición | *to leave a job* |
| el departamento de personal | *personnel department* |
| leer los clasificados | *to read the classified ads* |
| llenar la solicitud | *to fill out an application* |
| manejar un departamento | *to manage a department* |
| las obligaciones | *duties* |
| organizar | *to organize* |
| la posición | *position, job* |
| presentarse para una entrevista | *to go on an interview* |
| el resumé | *résumé* |
| tener éxito | *to be successful* |
| vender | *to sell* |
| vivir | *to live* |

# LESSON 27
## EN EL CORREO
### At the Post Office

Diana:      Quiero enviar este paquete por vía aérea a
            Miami.
Agente:     ¿Sabe usted cuánto pesa?
Diana:      No lo he pesado.

Diana:      *I want to send this package by air mail to
            Miami.*
Agent:      *Do you know how much it weighs?*
Diana:      *I haven't weighed it.*

# NEW VOCABULARY

| | |
|---|---|
| asegurar | to insure |
| las cartas | letters |
| el cartero | mailman |
| la casilla | postal box |
| certificar | to register |
| comprar estampillas | to buy stamps |
| el correo | mail; post office |
| de primera clase | first class |
| devolver | to return |
| echar una carta al buzón | to put a letter into the mailbox |
| la entrega inmediata | special delivery |
| entregar | to deliver |
| enviar | to send |
| enviar un paquete | to send a package |
| el giro postal | postal money order |
| haber | to have |
| mandar un paquete al extranjero | to send a package abroad |
| pesar | to weigh |
| recoger el correo | to pick up the mail |
| la tarjeta postal | postal card; postcard |
| abierto/a | opened |
| dicho/a | said |
| escrito/a | written |
| hecho/a | done |
| puesto/a | put |
| visto/a | seen |

# LESSON 28
## EN LA PLAYA
### At the Beach

| | |
|---|---|
| Teresa: | Pasaremos las vacaciones en un hotel que da a la playa. |
| Esteban: | Hay una playa excelente con una arena blanquita no muy lejos de aquí. Hay varias piscinas también. |
| Teresa: | A nuestro Danielito le gusta mucho jugar en el agua. |
| Esteban: | ¡Claro! |

| | |
|---|---|
| Teresa: | *We'll spend our vacation at a hotel that's on the beach.* |
| Esteban: | *There is an excellent beach with the whitest sand not far from here. There are several pools as well.* |
| Teresa: | *Our little Danny likes to play in the water a lot.* |
| Esteban: | *Of course!* |

# NEW VOCABULARY

| | |
|---|---|
| ahorita | *right now* |
| la arena | *sand* |
| blanquita | *really white* |
| las diversiones acuáticas | *water activities* |
| estar de vacaciones | *to be on vacation* |
| hacer buceo | *to go scuba diving* |
| hacer esquí acuático | *to go water skiing* |
| hacer surf | *to go surfing* |
| ir a un balneario | *to go to a resort* |
| jugar en el agua | *to play in the water* |
| la loción bronceadora | *tanning lotion* |
| mañana | *tomorrow* |
| nadar en el mar | *to swim in the ocean* |
| pasar las vacaciones | *to spend (a/the) vacation* |
| la piscina | *swimming pool* |
| la playa | *beach* |
| el protector de sol | *sunscreen* |
| la quemadura | *sunburn* |
| el salvavidas | *life vest* |
| tomar el sol | *to sunbathe* |
| Voy a verlo mañana. | *I'm going to see you tomorrow.* |

# LESSON 29
## EN EL BANCO
### At the Bank

Patricia: Quiero abrir una cuenta corriente. ¿Cuánto tendré que pagar por la chequera y por cheque cobrado?

Roberto: Habrá cargos reducidos por cheque por seis meses.

Patricia: ¿Tienen ustedes representantes por todo el mundo?

Roberto: Para el final del año los tendremos.

Patricia: *I want to open a checking account. How much will I have to pay for the checkbook and each cashed check?*

Roberto: *There will be reduced check charges for six months.*

Patricia: *Do you have branches throughout the world?*

Roberto: *By the end of the year we will have them.*

# NEW VOCABULARY

| | |
|---|---|
| el banquero | banker |
| caber | to fit |
| el cajero | teller |
| el cajero automático | ATM |
| los cargos | charges |
| chequear el saldo | to check the balance |
| la chequera | checkbook |
| cobrar un cheque | to cash a check |
| la cuenta corriente | checking account |
| la cuenta de ahorros | savings account |
| depositar un cheque | to deposit a check |
| el estado de la cuenta | account statement |
| habrá | there will be |
| obtener un préstamo | to get a loan |
| la papeleta de depósito | deposit slip |
| para | for, in order to |
| por | for, through, along |
| por ciento | percent |
| por eso | for that reason |
| por favor | please |
| reducido/a | reduced |
| la/el representante | representative |
| sacar dinero | to withdraw money |
| la tasa de interés | interest rate |
| los trámites | procedures |
| vía aérea | air mail |

# LESSON 30
## EN LA AGENCIA DE CAMBIO
### At the Currency Exchange Office

Ramón:     Me gustaría cambiar unos cheques de
           viajero. ¿A cuánto está el cambio hoy?
Débora:    ¿Para qué cantidad de dinero?
Ramón:     Cambiaría mil dólares.
Débora:    El cambio está a dos el dólar.


Ramón:     *I would like to cash some traveler's checks.*
           *What is the exchange rate today?*
Débora:    *For what amount of money?*
Ramón:     *I would like to exchange one thousand*
           *dollars.*
Débora:    *The rate is two to the dollar.*

# NEW VOCABULARY

| | |
|---|---|
| ¿A cuánto está el cambio? | *What is the exchange rate?* |
| los billetes | *bills of currency* |
| cambiar moneda | *to change money* |
| el cambio | *exchange office* |
| la cantidad | *quantity* |
| los cheques de viajero | *traveler's checks* |
| cobrar una tarifa | *to charge a fee* |
| el dólar | *dollar* |
| el euro | *euro* |
| el efectivo | *cash* |
| endosar | *to endorse* |
| Haga favor de venir. | *Please come.* |
| firmar | *to sign* |
| las libras | *pounds* |
| Me gustaria . . . | *I would like . . .* |
| la moneda | *coins, currency* |
| dos al dólar | *two to the dollar* |
| poner la fecha | *to write the date* |
| la transacción en divisa | *a currency transaction* |
| los yenes | *yen (pl)* |

# LESSON 31
## EN LA COMISARÍA
### At the Police Station

| | |
|---|---|
| Catalina: | Nos asaltaron dos personas con máscaras. |
| Detective: | ¿Qué les quitaron? |
| Catalina: | Las carteras y los relojes. |
| Detective: | ¿Intentaron ustedes escapar o gritar "¡Socorro!"? |
| Catalina: | Nos asustaron tanto que no pudimos reaccionar. |
| Detective: | Felizmente, no se les ha hecho daño físico. |

| | |
|---|---|
| *Catalina:* | *We were mugged by two people in masks.* |
| *Detective:* | *What was taken from you?* |
| *Catalina:* | *Our wallets and watches.* |
| *Detective:* | *Did you try to escape or yell "Help!"?* |
| *Catalina:* | *We were so frightened by them that we couldn't react.* |
| *Detective:* | *Fortunately, no physical harm was done to you.* |

# NEW VOCABULARY

| | |
|---|---|
| asaltar | *to mug* |
| asustar | *to frighten* |
| la cartera | *wallet* |
| el crimen | *crime* |
| ¡Déjeme en paz! | *Leave me alone!* |
| el/la detective | *detective* |
| ¡Deténgalo! | *Stop him!* |
| en voz alta | *in a loud voice* |
| la estación de policía | *police station* |
| físico | *physical* |
| gritar | *to yell* |
| hacer daño | *to do harm* |
| hacer una declaración | *to make a statement* |
| intentar escapar | *to try to escape* |
| el ladrón | *thief* |
| ¡Manos arriba! | *Hands up!* |
| la máscara | *mask* |
| matar | *to kill* |
| la pistola | *gun, pistol* |
| prender al ladrón | *to arrest the thief* |
| los primeros socorros/auxilios | *first aid* |
| quitársele a uno | *to take something away from someone* |
| reaccionar | *to react* |
| el reloj | *watch* |
| resistir | *to resist* |
| robar | *to rob* |
| Se prohibe fumar. | *No smoking.* |
| ser asaltado/a | *to be mugged* |
| ¡Socorro! | *Help!* |
| la víctima de crimen | *crime victim* |

# LESSON 32
## MIRAR LA TELEVISIÓN
### Watching Television

Pablo:    Prefiero ver las noticias del canal educativo.
          Los niños nos pedirán que cambiemos el canal.
          Querrán ver una comedia o unos dibujos
          animados.

Elena:    No me gusta que se pongan ante la pantalla
          por más de una hora al día.

Pablo:    *I prefer to watch the news on the educational
          channel. The kids will ask us to change the
          channel. They will want to watch a comedy or
          some cartoons.*

Elena:    *I don't like them to sit in front of the screen for
          more than an hour a day.*

# NEW VOCABULARY

| | |
|---|---|
| apagar la televisión | *to turn off the TV* |
| el cable | *cable* |
| cambiar el canal | *to change the channel* |
| el canal educativo | *educational channel* |
| la cinta de vídeo | *video tape* |
| la comedia | *comedy* |
| los dibujos animados | *cartoons* |
| el disco antena | *satellite dish* |
| la emisión | *broadcast* |
| grabar | *to tape* |
| insistir | *to insist* |
| mirar la televisión | *to watch television* |
| las noticias | *news* |
| el noticiero | *newscast* |
| la (tele)novela | *soap opera* |
| la pantalla | *screen* |
| poner el televisor | *to put on the television* |
| preferir | *to prefer* |
| recomendar | *to recommend* |
| la red | *network* |
| sintonizar | *to tune in* |
| sugerir | *to suggest* |
| veinticuatro horas al día | *24 hours a day* |
| la videograbadora | *VCR* |

# LESSON 33
## EN EL CINE
### At the Movies

Arturo:     Espero que podamos ir al cine esta noche.

Vera:     Vamos a consultar la cartelera para ver que exhiben. Hay un festival de películas de María Félix.

Arturo:     A ti te encantan las películas románticas. ¿A qué hora comienza la función?

Vera:     A las ocho. ¡Vámonos!


Arturo:     *I hope we can go to the movies tonight.*

Vera:     *Let's check the movie listings to see what's playing. There is a María Félix film festival.*

Arturo:     *You like romantic films. At what time does the film begin?*

Vera:     *At eight o'clock. Let's go!*

# NEW VOCABULARY

| | |
|---|---|
| el asiento adelante | seat in front |
| el asiento atrás | seat in the back |
| el cine | movie theater |
| consultar la cartelera | to check the listings |
| el cortometraje | short film |
| doblar | to dub |
| encantarle a uno | to like |
| exhibir una película | to show a film |
| el festival de películas | film festival |
| el film | film |
| el film a colores | color film |
| el film en blanco y negro | black and white film |
| el film extranjero | foreign film |
| la función | showing, session |
| las funciones seguidas | continuous showing |
| el largometraje | feature length |
| las leyendas | subtitles |
| el misterio | mystery |
| la película romántica | romantic film |
| el público | audience |
| el refresco | soft drink |
| las rosetas (de maíz); palomitas | popcorn |

# LESSON 34
## LOS DEPORTES
### Sports

Emilio:     Dudo que haya otro deporte más exigente y emocionante que el fútbol. Para el espectador no hay otro deporte que se compare con el fútbol.

Carmen:    Los futbolistas se dedican al cuidado del cuerpo. ¡Cómo a mí me gustaría pasar las horas de trabajo en un campo de fútbol!

Emilio:     *I doubt that there is another sport more demanding and thrilling than soccer. For the spectator there is no other sport that compares to soccer.*

Carmen:    *Soccer players are dedicated to the care of their bodies. How I would like to spend my working hours on a soccer field!*

# NEW VOCABULARY

| | |
|---|---|
| la arena | arena |
| el atletismo | track and field sports |
| el béisbol | baseball |
| los boxeadores | boxers |
| el boxeo | boxing |
| el campo de fútbol | soccer field |
| la cancha de tenis | tennis court |
| compararse con | to compare oneself with |
| el cuidado del cuerpo | care of the body |
| dedicarse a | to dedicate oneself to |
| el deporte | sport |
| los deportistas | athletes |
| dudar | to doubt |
| emocionante | exciting |
| entrenarse | to train |
| el equipo | team |
| el espectador | spectator |
| el estadio | stadium |
| exigente | demanding |
| el fútbol | soccer |
| el golf | golf |
| el/la hincha | fan |
| jugar al deporte | to play a sport |
| la liga | league |
| negar | to deny |
| el partido | game |
| pasar horas | to spend hours |
| la puntuación | score |
| quizás | maybe |
| tal vez | perhaps; maybe |
| el tenis | tennis |

# LESSON 35
## EN EL HOTEL
### At the Hotel

| Gerente: | Tengo aquí su reservación. Una habitación doble, con baño particular y aire acondicionado. |
| Miguel: | Es preferible que me den un cuarto que está en un piso bajo. |
| Gerente: | La habitación cuatrocientos tres estará lista después de que la limpien. Aquí tiene la carta-llave. |

| Manager: | I have your reservation here. A double room, with private bath and air-conditioning. |
| Miguel: | I would prefer that you give me a room on a lower floor. |
| Manager: | Room 403 will be ready after they clean it. Here's the card key. |

# NEW VOCABULARY

| | |
|---|---|
| el aire acondicionado | *air-conditioning* |
| antes de que | *before* |
| el baño particular | *private bath* |
| el botones | *bellhop* |
| la caja de valores | *safety deposit box* |
| la carta-llave | *card key* |
| después de que | *after* |
| Es evidente. | *It's evident.* |
| Es imposible. | *It's impossible.* |
| Es necesario/a. | *It's necessary.* |
| Es posible. | *It's possible.* |
| Es preferible. | *It's preferable.* |
| estar listo/a | *to be ready* |
| guardar el equipaje | *to store baggage* |
| la habitación | *room* |
| la habitación doble | *double room* |
| hacer una reservación | *to make a reservation* |
| hospedarse; quedarse en un hotel | *to stay at a hotel* |
| la maleta | *suitcase* |
| el piso | *floor* |
| el piso bajo | *ground floor* |
| la recepción | *lobby* |
| el servicio de cuarto | *room service* |
| Tengo aquí . . . | *Here is . . .* |

# SUPPLEMENTAL VOCABULARY LISTS

Use these thematically organized lists to master basic vocabulary for 18 different essential situations. Each vocabulary item, along with its translation, is recorded on CD 8 of your program.

## 1. Weather

| | |
|---|---|
| el tiempo | *weather* |
| Está lloviendo. | *It's raining.* |
| Está nevando. | *It's snowing.* |
| Está granizando. | *It's hailing.* |
| Hace viento. | *It's windy.* |
| Hace calor. | *It's hot.* |
| Hace frío. | *It's cold.* |
| Hace sol. | *It's sunny.* |
| Está nublado. | *It's cloudy.* |
| Hace muy buen tiempo. | *It's beautiful.* |
| la tormenta | *storm* |
| el viento | *wind* |
| el sol | *sun* |
| el trueno | *thunder* |
| el relámpago | *lightening* |
| el huracán | *hurricane* |
| la temperatura | *temperature* |
| el grado | *degree* |
| la lluvia | *rain* |
| la nieve | *snow* |
| la nube | *cloud* |
| la niebla | *fog* |
| la niebla tóxica/el smog | *smog* |
| el paraguas | *umbrella* |

## 2. Food

| | |
|---|---|
| la comida | *food* |
| la cena | *dinner* |
| el almuerzo | *lunch* |
| el desayuno | *breakfast* |

| | |
|---|---|
| la carne | meat, beef |
| el pollo | chicken |
| la carne de cerdo | pork |
| el pescado | fish |
| el camarón/la gamba | shrimp |
| la langosta | lobster |
| el pan | bread |
| el huevo | egg |
| el queso | cheese |
| el arroz | rice |
| la verdura/el vegetal | vegetable |
| la lechuga | lettuce |
| el tomate | tomato |
| la zanahoria | carrot |
| el pepino | cucumber |
| el pimiento | pepper |
| la fruta | fruit |
| la manzana | apple |
| la naranja | orange |
| el plátano/la banana | banana |
| la pera | pear |
| las uvas | grapes |
| la bebida | drink |
| el agua | water |
| la leche | milk |
| el jugo/el zumo | juice |
| el café | coffee |
| el té | tea |
| el vino | wine |
| la cerveza | beer |
| el refresco | soft drink/soda |
| la sal | salt |
| la pimienta | pepper |
| el azúcar | sugar |
| la miel | honey |
| frío/caliente | hot/cold |
| dulce/amargo | sweet/sour |

### 3. People

| | |
|---|---|
| la gente | *people* |
| la persona | *person* |
| el hombre | *man* |
| la mujer | *woman* |
| el adulto/la adulta | *adult* |
| el niño/la niña | *child* |
| el niño/el chico | *boy* |
| la niña/la chica | *girl* |
| la/el adolescente | *teenager* |
| alto/bajo | *tall/short* |
| viejo/joven | *old/young* |
| gordo/delgado | *fat/thin* |
| simpático/antipático | *friendly/unfriendly* |
| alegre/triste | *happy/sad* |
| bonito/feo | *beautiful/ugly* |
| enfermo/saludable | *sick/healthy* |
| fuerte/débil | *strong/weak* |
| famoso | *famous* |
| inteligente | *intelligent* |
| dotado | *talented* |

### 4. At home

| | |
|---|---|
| en casa | *at home* |
| casa | *house* |
| el apartamento | *apartment* |
| la habitación | *room* |
| la sala | *living room* |
| el comedor | *dining room* |
| la cocina | *kitchen* |
| el dormitorio | *bedroom* |
| el baño | *bathroom* |
| el vestíbulo | *hall* |
| el armario | *closet* |
| la ventana | *window* |
| la puerta | *door* |
| la mesa | *table* |
| la silla | *chair* |

| | |
|---|---|
| el sofá | sofa/couch |
| la cortina | curtain |
| la alfombra | carpet |
| el televisor | television |
| el lector de cd | cd player |
| la lámpara | lamp |
| el lector de dvd | DVD player |
| el sistema de sonido | sound system |
| la pintura/el cuadro | painting/picture |
| el estante | shelf |
| las escaleras | stairs |
| el techo | ceiling |
| la pared | wall |
| el suelo | floor |
| pequeño/grande | big/small |
| nuevo/viejo | new/old |
| madera/de madera | wood/wooden |
| plástico/hecho de plástico | plastic/made of plastic |

## 5. The human body

| | |
|---|---|
| el cuerpo humano | the human body |
| la cabeza | head |
| la cara | face |
| la frente | forehead |
| el ojo | eye |
| la ceja | eyebrow |
| las pestañas | eyelashes |
| la oreja | ear |
| la nariz | nose |
| la boca | mouth |
| el diente | tooth |
| la lengua | tongue |
| la mejilla | cheek |
| la barbilla | chin |
| el pelo | hair |
| el cuello | neck |
| el pecho | chest |
| el pecho/el seno | breast |
| los hombros | shoulders |

| | |
|---|---|
| el brazo | arm |
| el codo | elbow |
| la muñeca | wrist |
| la mano | hand |
| el estómago/el abdomen | stomach/abdomen |
| el pene | penis |
| la vagina | vagina |
| la pierna | leg |
| la rodilla | knee |
| el tobillo | ankle |
| el pie | foot |
| el dedo | finger |
| el dedo del pie | toe |
| la piel | skin |
| la sangre | blood |
| el cerebro | brain |
| el corazón | heart |
| los pulmones | lungs |
| el hueso | bone |
| el músculo | muscle |
| el tendón | tendon |

## 6. Travel and tourism

| | |
|---|---|
| viaje y turismo | travel and tourism |
| la/el turista | tourist |
| el hotel | hotel |
| el hostal | youth hostel |
| la recepción | reception desk |
| registrarse | to check in |
| pagar la cuenta | to check out |
| la reserva/la reservación | reservation |
| el pasaporte | passport |
| el recorrido por autobús | tour bus |
| la visita guiada | guided tour |
| la cámara | camera |
| el centro de información | information center |
| el mapa/el plano | map |
| el folleto | brochure |
| el monumento | monument |

| visitar los lugares de interés | to go sightseeing |
| hacer una foto | to take a picture |
| ¿Puedes hacernos una foto? | Can you take our picture? |

## 7. In the office

| en la oficina | in the office |
| la oficina/el despacho | office |
| el escritorio | desk |
| la computadora/el ordenador | computer |
| el teléfono | telephone |
| el fax | fax machine |
| el estante | bookshelf |
| el armario | filing cabinet |
| la carpeta/el archivo | file |
| el jefe/la jefa | boss |
| el colega/la colega | colleague |
| el empleado/la empleada | employee |
| el personal/la plantilla | staff |
| la compañía | company |
| el negocio | business |
| la fábrica | factory |
| la sala de conferencias | meeting room |
| la reunión | meeting |
| la cita | appointment |
| el salario | salary |
| el trabajo | job |
| ocupado | busy |
| trabajar | to work |
| ganar | to earn |

## 8. At school

| en la escuela | at school |
| la escuela | school |
| la universidad | university |
| el aula | classroom |
| el curso | course |
| el maestro/la maestra | teacher |
| el profesor/la profesora | professor |

| el estudiante/la estudiante | student |
| la asignatura | subject |
| el cuaderno | notebook |
| el libro de texto | textbook |
| las matemáticas | math |
| la historia | history |
| la química | chemistry |
| la biología | biology |
| la literatura | literature |
| la lengua | language |
| el arte | art |
| la música | music |
| la gimnasia | gym |
| el receso | recess |
| el examen/la prueba | test |
| la nota | grade |
| las calificaciones | report card |
| el diploma | diploma |
| el título | degree |
| difícil/fácil | difficult/easy |
| estudiar | to study |
| aprender | to learn |
| aprobar | to pass |
| suspender | to fail |

## 9. Sports and recreation

| deportes y recreo | sports and recreation |
| el fútbol/el fútbol americano | soccer/football |
| el baloncesto | basketball |
| el béisbol | baseball |
| el hockey | hockey |
| el tenis | tennis |
| el juego/el partido | game |
| el equipo | team |
| el estadio | stadium |
| el entrenador/la entrenadora | coach |
| el jugador/la jugadora | player |
| el campeón/la campeona | champion |
| la pelota/el balón | ball |

| | |
|---|---|
| hacer excursionismo/hacer senderismo | *to go hiking* |
| ir de camping | *to go camping* |
| jugar un deporte | *to play a sport* |
| jugar un partido | *to play a game* |
| ganar | *to win* |
| perder | *to lose* |
| empatar | *to draw/tie* |
| los naipes/las cartas | *cards* |
| el billar | *pool/billiards* |

## 10. Nature

| | |
|---|---|
| la naturaleza | *nature* |
| el árbol | *tree* |
| la flor | *flower* |
| el bosque | *forest* |
| la montaña | *mountain* |
| el campo | *field* |
| el río | *river* |
| el lago | *lake* |
| el océano | *ocean* |
| el mar | *sea* |
| la playa | *beach* |
| el desierto | *desert* |
| la roca | *rock* |
| la arena | *sand* |
| el cielo | *sky* |
| el sol | *sun* |
| la luna | *moon* |
| la estrella | *star* |
| el agua | *water* |
| la tierra | *land* |
| la planta | *plant* |
| el cerro/la colina | *hill* |
| el estanque | *pond* |

## 11. Computers and the internet

| | |
|---|---|
| las computadoras y la Internet | *computers and the internet* |
| la computadora/el ordenador | *computer* |
| el teclado | *keyboard* |
| el monitor/la pantalla | *monitor/screen* |
| la impresora | *printer* |
| el ratón | *mouse* |
| el módem | *modem* |
| la memoria | *memory* |
| el cd rom | *CD-ROM* |
| el lector de cd rom | *CD-ROM drive* |
| el archivo | *file* |
| el documento | *document* |
| el cable | *cable* |
| línea de suscriptor/abonado digital (adsl) | *DSL* |
| la Internet | *internet* |
| el sitio web | *website* |
| la página web | *webpage* |
| el correo electrónico | *e-mail* |
| el espacio para charla/ el chat | *chat room* |
| el registro del web | *weblog (blog)* |
| el mensaje instantáneo | *instant message* |
| el documento adjunto | *attachment* |
| enviar un correo electrónico/correo-e | *to send an e-mail* |
| enviar un documento adjunto | *to send a file* |
| pasar/retransmitir | *to forward* |
| contestar | *to reply* |
| eliminar | *to delete* |
| guardar un documento | *to save a document* |
| abrir un documento | *to open a file* |
| cerrar un documento | *to close a file* |
| adjuntar un documento | *to attach a file* |

## 12. Family and relationships

| | |
|---|---|
| familia y relaciones | *family and relationships* |
| la madre | *mother* |
| el padre | *father* |
| el hijo | *son* |
| la hija | *daughter* |
| la hermana | *sister* |
| la/el bebé | *baby* |
| el hermano | *brother* |
| el esposo/marido | *husband* |
| la esposa/mujer | *wife* |
| la tía | *aunt* |
| el tío | *uncle* |
| la abuela | *grandmother* |
| el abuelo | *grandfather* |
| el primo/la prima | *cousin* |
| la suegra | *mother-in-law* |
| el suegro | *father-in-law* |
| la madrastra | *stepmother* |
| el padrastro | *stepfather* |
| el hijastro | *stepson* |
| la hijastra | *stepdaughter* |
| el novio | *boyfriend* |
| la novia | *girlfriend* |
| el prometido/la prometida | *fiancé(e)* |
| el amigo/la amiga | *friend* |
| el/la pariente | *relative* |
| querer/amar | *to love* |
| conocer | *to know (a person)* |
| encontrarse con | *to meet* |
| casarse con | *to marry* |
| divorciarse de | *to divorce (someone)* |
| divorciarse | *to get a divorce* |
| heredar | *to inherit* |

## 13. On the job

| | |
|---|---|
| empleos | *jobs* |
| el policía/la mujer policía | *policeman/policewoman* |

| | |
|---|---|
| el abogado/la abogada | lawyer |
| el doctor/la doctora | doctor |
| el ingeniero/la ingeniera | engineer |
| el hombre de negocios/ | businessman/ |
| la mujer de negocios | businesswoman |
| el vendedor/la vendedora | salesman/saleswoman |
| el maestro/la maestra | teacher |
| el profesor/la profesora | professor |
| el banquero/la banquera | banker |
| el arquitecto/la arquitecta | architect |
| el veterinario/la veterinaria | veterinarian |
| el dentista/la dentista | dentist |
| el carpintero/la carpintera | carpenter |
| el obrero/la obrera | construction worker |
| el taxista/la taxista | taxi driver |
| el artista/la artista | artist |
| el escritor/la escritora | writer |
| el fontanero/la fontanera | plumber |
| el electricista/la electricista | electrician |
| el periodista/la periodista | journalist |
| el actor/la actriz | actor/actress |
| el músico/la música | musician |
| el granjero/la granjera | farmer |
| el secretario/la secretaria, | |
| la asistente/el asistente | secretary/assistant |
| parado/parada | unemployed |
| jubilado/jubilada | retired |
| a tiempo completo | full-time |
| a tiempo parcial | part-time |
| el trabajo fijo | steady job |
| el trabajo de verano | summer job |

## 14. Clothing

| | |
|---|---|
| la ropa | clothing |
| la camisa | shirt |
| los pantalones | pants |
| los vaqueros/los tejanos | jeans |
| la camiseta | T-shirt |

| los zapatos | shoes |
| los calcetines | socks |
| el cinturón | belt |
| las zapatillas deportivas | sneaker/tennis shoe |
| el vestido | dress |
| la falda | skirt |
| la blusa | blouse |
| el traje | suit |
| el sombrero | hat |
| los guantes | gloves |
| la bufanda | scarf |
| la chaqueta | jacket |
| el abrigo | coat |
| el pendiente | earring |
| la pulsera | bracelet |
| el collar | necklace |
| las gafas | eyeglasses |
| las gafas de sol | sunglasses |
| el reloj | watch |
| el anillo | ring |
| los calzoncillos | underpants |
| la camisilla/la camiseta | undershirt |
| el bañador | bathing trunks |
| el traje de baño | bathing suit |
| el pijama | pajamas |
| el algodón | cotton |
| el cuero | leather |
| la seda | silk |
| la talla | size |
| llevar | to wear |

## 15. In the kitchen

| en la cocina | in the kitchen |
| la nevera | refrigerator |
| el fregadero | (kitchen) sink |
| el mostrador | counter |
| la cocina | stove |
| el horno | oven |
| el microondas | microwave |

| | |
|---|---|
| el aparador | cupboard |
| el cajón | drawer |
| el plato | plate |
| la taza | cup |
| el cuenco/tazón | bowl |
| el vaso | glass |
| la cuchara | spoon |
| el cuchillo | knife |
| la lata | can |
| la caja | box |
| la botella | bottle |
| el bote/cartón | carton |
| la cafetera | coffeemaker |
| la tetera | teakettle |
| la batidora | blender |
| la plancha | iron |
| la tabla de planchar | ironing board |
| la escoba | broom |
| el lavaplatos | dishwasher |
| la lavadora | washing machine |
| la secadora | dryer |
| cocinar | to cook |
| lavar los platos | to do the dishes |
| lavar la ropa | to do the laundry |
| detergente de vajilla | dishwashing detergent |
| detergente de ropa | laundry detergent |
| lejía | bleach |
| limpio/sucio | clean/dirty |

## 16. In the bathroom

| | |
|---|---|
| en el baño | in the bathroom |
| el inodoro | toilet |
| el lavabo | sink (wash basin) |
| la bañera | bathtub |
| la ducha | shower |
| el espejo | mirror |
| el botiquín | medicine cabinet |
| la toalla | towel |
| el papel higiénico | toilet paper |

| el champú | shampoo |
| el jabón | soap |
| el gel de baño | bath gel |
| la crema de afeitar | shaving cream |
| la navaja de afeitar | razor |
| lavarse | to wash onself |
| ducharse/bañarse | to take a shower/bath |
| afeitarse | to shave |
| la colonia | cologne |
| el perfume | perfume |
| el desodorante | deodorant |
| el vendaje | bandage |
| el polvo | powder |

## 17. Around town

| por la ciudad | around town |
| el pueblo | town |
| la ciudad | city |
| la aldea | village |
| el carro/el coche/el automóvil | car |
| el autobús | bus |
| el tren | train |
| el taxi | taxi |
| el subterráneo/el metro | subway/metro |
| el tráfico | traffic |
| el edificio | building |
| el edificio de apartamentos | apartment building |
| la biblioteca | library |
| el restaurante | restaurant |
| la tienda | store |
| la calle | street |
| el parque | park |
| la estación de ferrocarril | train station |
| el aeropuerto | airport |
| el avión | airplane |
| la intersección | intersection |
| la farola | lamppost |
| la luz de la calle | streetlight |
| el banco | bank |

| | |
|---|---|
| la iglesia | church |
| el templo | temple |
| la mezquita | mosque |
| la acera | sidewalk |
| la panadería | bakery |
| la carnicería | butcher shop |
| la cafetería | café/coffee shop |
| la farmacia | drugstore/pharmacy |
| el supermercado | supermarket |
| el mercado | market |
| la zapatería | shoe store |
| la tienda de ropa | clothing store |
| la tienda de electrodomésticos | electronics store |
| la librería | bookstore |
| la tienda por departamentos | department store |
| el alcalde | mayor |
| el ayuntamiento/la alcaldía | city hall/municipal building |
| comprar | to buy |
| ir de compras | to go shopping |
| cerca/lejos | near/far |
| urbano | urban |
| suburbano | suburban |
| rural | rural |

## 18. Entertainment

| | |
|---|---|
| el entretenimiento | entertainment |
| la película | movie/film |
| ir al cine | to go to the movies |
| ver una película | to see a movie |
| el teatro | theater |
| ver una obra de teatro | to see a play |
| la ópera | opera |
| el concierto | concert |
| el club | club |
| el circo | circus |
| la entrada/el boleto | ticket |
| el museo | museum |

| | |
|---|---|
| la galería | *gallery* |
| la pintura | *painting* |
| la escultura | *sculpture* |
| el programa de televisión | *television program* |
| mirar la televisón | *to watch television* |
| la comedia | *comedy* |
| el documental | *documentary* |
| la obra dramática | *drama* |
| el libro | *book* |
| la revista | *magazine* |
| leer un libro | *to read a book* |
| leer una revista | *to read a magazine* |
| escuchar música | *to listen to music* |
| la canción | *song* |
| la banda/el conjunto | *band* |
| las noticias | *the news* |
| el programa de entrevistas | *talk show* |
| cambiar de canales | *to change channels* |
| divertirse | *to have fun* |
| estar aburrido | *to be bored* |
| gracioso | *funny* |
| interesante | *interesting* |
| emocionante | *exciting* |
| espantoso | *scary* |
| fiesta | *party* |
| restaurante | *restaurant* |
| ir a una fiesta | *to go to a party* |
| tener una fiesta | *to have a party* |
| bailar | *to dance* |

# GRAMMAR SUMMARY

## 1. The Definite Article (the)

|  | SINGULAR | PLURAL |
|---|---|---|
| MASCULINE | el | los |
| FEMININE | la | las |

## 2. The Indefinite Article (a, an)

|  | SINGULAR | PLURAL |
|---|---|---|
| MASCULINE | un | unos |
| FEMININE | una | unas |

## 3. Gender of Nouns

All Spanish nouns are either masculine or feminine. Some words can be grouped by gender, but there are exceptions and it is best to learn the word with its appropriate article.

Masculine words: nouns that end in -o, -r, -n, and -l; names of items in nature (e.g., mountains); days of the week and months; words of Greek origin ending in -ma, -pa, or -ta; verbs, adjectives, etc. used as nouns.

Feminine words: nouns that end in -a, -dad, -tad, -tud, -ción, -sión, -ez, -umbre, and -ie; names of cities, towns, and fruits.

## 4. Number of Nouns

To form the plural of nouns ending in a vowel, add -s. For nouns ending in a consonant or a stressed í or ú, add -es. Nouns ending in -z change to -c in the plural; e.g., happy children—niños felices.

## 5. Adjectives

All adjectives must agree in number and gender with the nouns they modify, or describe. For use with plural nouns, add -s or -es (if it ends in a consonant) to the adjective. An adjective ending in -o in its masculine form ends in -a in its feminine form; e.g., the rich woman—la mujer rica. For certain adjectives that end in a consonant or a vowel other than -o in the masculine form, add -a for the feminine form. Other adjectives have the same form for both genders.

Note that, in Spanish, adjectives usually follow the noun.

## 6. Subject Pronouns

| | |
|---|---|
| yo | *I* |
| tú | *you (infml sg)* |
| él | *he* |
| ella | *she* |
| usted (Ud.) | *you (fml sg)* |
| nosotros/nosotras | *we* |
| vosotros/vosotras | *you (infml pl)* |
| ustedes (Uds.) | *you (fml pl)* |
| ellos/ellas | *they* |

*Usted* and *ustedes* are treated as if they were third person pronouns, though in meaning, they are second person (addressee) pronouns. *Vosotros/-as* is not used in Latin America, so *ustedes* is used as both familiar and polite plural.

Subject pronouns are often omitted since the verbal endings show who or what the subject is.

## 7. Direct Object Pronouns

| | |
|---|---|
| me | *me* |
| te | *you (infml sg)* |
| lo | *him, it* |
| la | *her, it* |
| lo/la | *you (fml sg)* |
| nos | *us* |
| os | *you (infml pl)* |
| los/las | *them, you (fml pl)* |

## 8. Indirect Object Pronouns

| | |
|---|---|
| me | *to me* |
| te | *to you (infml sg)* |
| le | *to him, to her, to it, to you (fml sg)* |
| nos | *to us* |
| os | *to you (infml pl)* |
| les | *to them, to you (fml pl)* |

## 9. Reflexive Pronouns

| | |
|---|---|
| me | *myself* |
| te | *yourself (infml sg)* |
| se | *him/her/itself, yourself (fml sg)* |
| nos | *ourselves* |
| os | *yourselves (infml pl)* |
| se | *themselves; yourselves (fml pl)* |

## 10. Possessive Adjectives

| | |
|---|---|
| mi(s) | *my* |
| tu(s) | *your (infml sg)* |
| su(s) | *his, her, its, your (fml sg)* |
| nuestro(s)/nuestra(s) | *our* |
| vuestro(s)/vuestra(s) | *your (infml pl)* |
| su(s) | *their, your (fml pl)* |

## 11. Possessive Pronouns

| | |
|---|---|
| mío(s) | *mine* |
| tuyo(s) | *yours (infml sg)* |
| suyo(s) | *his, hers, its, yours (fml sg)* |
| nuestro(s)/nuestra(s) | *ours* |
| vuestro(s)/vuestra(s) | *yours (infml pl)* |
| su(s) | *theirs, yours (fml pl)* |

## 12. Pronouns Following Prepositions

Use the subject pronouns following prepositions, except in the *yo* and *tú* forms, where *mí* and *ti* should be used instead. The same is true for reflexive pronouns, but use *sí* as the third person (singular and plural) pronoun in addition. After *con* (with), use the special forms *-migo*, *-tigo*, and *-sigo* instead of *mí*, *ti*, or *sí*.

## 13. Demonstratives
### (THIS, THESE; THAT, THOSE; THIS ONE, THAT ONE)

### A. THE ADJECTIVES: THIS, THESE

| | SINGULAR | PLURAL |
|---|---|---|
| MASCULINE | este | estos |
| FEMININE | esta | estas |

### B. THE ADJECTIVES: THAT, THOSE

| | SINGULAR | PLURAL |
|---|---|---|
| MASCULINE | ese | esos |
| FEMININE | esa | esas |

## C. THE ADJECTIVES: THAT, THOSE (FARTHER REMOVED)

| | SINGULAR | PLURAL |
|---|---|---|
| MASCULINE | aquel | aquellos |
| FEMININE | aquella | aquellas |

To form the pronouns, simply add an accent to the first *e* in the word, as in *No me gusta éste* (I don't like this one). There are also neuter pronouns used for general ideas or situations: *esto, eso, aquello.*

## 14. Adverbs

Form adverbs simply by adding *-mente* (which corresponds to *-ly* in English) to the feminine form of an adjective, as in *obviamente* (obviously).

## 15. Double Negatives

| nada | nothing |
|---|---|
| nadie | no one |
| nunca | never |
| jamás | never |
| ni . . . ni | neither . . . nor |
| tampoco | neither |
| ninguno/a | no, none, not any |

When these negatives precede the verb, they are used alone, but when they follow the verb, they must be used in conjunction with *no.*

## 16. Comparison

Form comparative expressions using *más* (more) and *menos* (less) with adjectives and adverbs; e.g., *Juan es más grande que Pepe* (Juan is bigger than Pepe), *Juan corre más rápido que Pepe* (Juan runs faster than Pepe), *Juan es menos famoso* (Juan is less famous). Use *de* instead of *que* to mean "than" before numbers.

To make equal comparisons, use the expressions *tan . . . como* (before adjectives and adverbs) and *tanto . . . como* (before nouns, with which *tanto* must agree). For example, *Juan es tan grande como Pepe* (Juan is as big as Pepe), *Juan tiene tanto dinero como Pepe* (Juan has as much money as Pepe).

Form superlatives by using an article or pronoun (*el* for adjectives, *lo* for adverbs) with the comparative expressions; e.g., *Juan es el más grande* (Juan is the biggest), *Pepe es el menos grande* (Pepe is the smallest), *Juan corre el más rápido* (Juan runs the fastest).

## 17. Irregular Comparatives

| ADJECTIVE | ADVERB | COMPARATIVE |
|---|---|---|
| bueno (*good*) | bien (*well*) | mejor (*better*) |
| malo (*bad*) | mal (*badly*) | peor (*worse*) |
| mucho (*much*) | mucho (*much*) | más (*more*) |
| poco (*little*) | poco (*little*) | menos (*less*) |
| grande (*big, great*) | | más grande (*bigger*) |
| | | BUT mayor (*older*) |
| pequeño (*small*) | | más pequeño (*smaller*) |
| | | BUT menor (*younger*) |

## 18. Relative Pronouns

| | |
|---|---|
| que | *that, who, which* |
| quien | *who(m)* |
| el, la, los, las cuales | *who, which* |
| el, la, los, las que | *who, which, the one(s) that/who* |
| lo que | *what, which (refers to an entire idea)* |
| cuyo, -a, -os, -as | *whose (relative adjective)* |

## 19. Prepositions

| | | | |
|---|---|---|---|
| a | *to* | hacia | *towards* |
| ante | *before, in front of* | hasta | *until* |
| bajo | *under* | para | *for* |
| con | *with* | por | *for* |
| contra | *against* | según | *according to* |
| de | *of, from, by* | sin | *without* |
| desde | *from* | sobre | *on top of* |
| en | *in* | tras | *behind* |
| entre | *between, among* | | |

## 20. Contractions

de + el = del
a + el = al

## 21. The Simple Verb Forms

1. To form the **present indicative**—*presente de indicativo* of regular verbs, add the following endings to the stem of the infinitive*:

FOR -*AR* VERBS: -*o*, -*as*, -*a*, -*amos*, -*áis*, -*an*\*\*
FOR -*ER* VERBS: -*o*, -*es*, -*e*, -*emos*, -*éis*, -*en*
FOR -*IR* VERBS: -*o*, -*es*, -*e*, -*imos*, -*ís*, -*en*

2. To form the **preterite**—*pretérito* of regular verbs, add the following endings to the stem of the infinitive:

FOR -*AR* VERBS: -*é*, -*aste*, -*ó*, -*amos*, -*asteis*, -*aron*
FOR -*ER* AND -*IR* VERBS: -*í*, -*iste*, -*ió*, -*imos*, -*isteis*, -*ieron*

Several verbs that are irregular in the preterite follow a pattern. Conjugate them in the following manner:

*tener*—to have: *tuve, tuviste, tuvo, tuvimos, tuvisteis, tuvieron*
*estar*—to be: *estuve* . . .
*andar*—to walk: *anduve* . . .
*haber*—to have: *hube* . . .
*poder*—to be able: *pude* . . .
*poner*—to put: *puse* . . .
*saber*—to know: *supe* . . .
*caber*—to fit: *cupe* . . .
*querer*—to want: *quise* . . .
*venir*—to come: *vine* . . .
*hacer*—to do, make: *hice, hiciste, hizo* . . .
*decir*—to say, tell: *dije* . . . *dijeron*
*traer*—to bring: *traje* . . . *trajeron*
*producir*—to produce: *produje* . . . *produjeron*

3. To form the **imperfect**—*imperfecto* of regular verbs, add the following endings to the stem of the infinitive:

FOR -*AR* VERBS: -*aba*, -*abas*, -*aba*, -*ábamos*, -*abais*, -*aban*
FOR -*ER* AND -*IR* VERBS: -*ía*, -*ías*, -*ía*, -*íamos*, -*íais*, -*ían*

There are only three irregular verbs in the imperfect:

*ser*—to be: *era, eras, era, éramos, erais, eran*
*ir*—to go: *iba, ibas, iba, íbamos, ibais, iban*
*ver*—to see: *veía, veías, veía, veíamos, veíais, veían*

---

\*The stem is formed by dropping the infinitival endings -*ar*, -*er*, and -*ir*.

\*\*The endings will always be presented according to subject person and number in the following order: *yo, tú, él/ella/usted, nosotros/-as, vosotros/-as, ellos/ellas/ustedes*.

4. To form the **future**—*futuro* of regular verbs, add the following endings to the entire infinitive:

FOR *-AR*, *-ER*, AND *-IR* VERBS: *-é, -ás, -á, -emos, -éis, -án*

5. To form the **conditional**—*potencial simple* of regular verbs, add the following endings to the entire infinitive:

FOR *-AR*, *-ER*, AND *-IR* VERBS: *-ía, -ías, -ía, -íamos, -íais, -ían*

The same set of verbs are irregular in the future and conditional. Add the regular endings to the following stems:

*tener*—to have: *tendr-*
*venir*—to come: *vendr-*
*poner*—to put, place: *pondr-*
*salir*—to leave: *saldr-*
*valer*—to be worth: *valdr-*
*poder*—to be able: *podr-*
*saber*—to know: *sabr-*
*haber*—to have: *habr-*
*caber*—to fit: *cabr-*
*hacer*—to do, make: *har-*
*decir*—to say, tell: *dir-*
*querer*—to want: *querr-*

6. To form the **present subjunctive**—*presente del subjuntivo* of regular verbs and many irregular ones, add the following endings to the *yo* form of the present indicative after dropping the *-o:*

FOR *-AR* VERBS: *-e, -es, -e, -emos, -éis, -en*
FOR *-ER* AND *-IR* VERBS: *-a, -as, -a, -amos, -áis, -an*

7. To form the **past** (imperfect) **subjunctive**—*imperfecto del subjuntivo* of both regular and irregular verbs, add the following endings to the *ellos/ellas/ustedes* (third person plural) form of the preterite after dropping the *-ron:*

FOR *-AR*, *-ER*, AND *-IR* VERBS: *-ra, -ras, -ra, -ramos, -rais, -ran*
OR: *-se, -ses, -se, -semos, -seis, -sen*

The *nosotros/-as* (first person plural) form has an accent on the vowel directly before the ending, e.g., *habláramos.*

## 22. The Compound Verb Forms

1. To form **progressive**—*progresivo* verb forms, conjugate the verb *estar*—to be in the appropriate tense (either the present or the imperfect; see verb charts) and add the present participle. Form the present participle of most verbs by adding the following endings to the stem of the infinitive:

FOR -*AR* VERBS: -*ando*
FOR -*ER* AND -*IR* VERBS: -*iendo*

2. To form **perfect**—*perfecto* verb forms, conjugate the auxiliary verb *haber*—to have in the appropriate tense (the present indicative, the imperfect, the preterite, the future, the conditional, the present subjunctive, and the past subjunctive; see verb charts) and add the past participle. Form the past participle of most verbs by adding the following endings to the stem of the infinitive:

FOR -*AR* VERBS: -*ado*
FOR -*ER* AND -*IR* VERBS: -*ido*

The irregular past participles are:

*abrir*—to open: *abierto*
*cubrir*—to cover: *cubierto*
*morir*—to die: *muerto*
*volver*—to return: *vuelto*
*poner*—to put, place: *puesto*
*ver*—to see: *visto*
*escribir*—to write: *escrito*
*romper*—to break: *roto*
*decir*—to say, tell: *dicho*
*hacer*—to do, make: *hecho*

## 23. The Imperative/Commands

A sample conjugation using *hablar*—to speak:

| | |
|---|---|
| fam. sing. affirm. *habla* | pol. sing. affirm. *hable* |
| fam. pl. affirm. *hablad* | pol. pl. affirm. *hablen* |
| fam. sing. neg. *no hables* | pol. sing. neg. *no hable* |
| fam. pl. neg. *no habléis* | pol. pl. neg. *no hablen* |

1. To form familiar (informal) singular (*tú*) affirmative commands for most verbs, use the *él/ella/usted* (third person singular) form of the present indicative.

2. To form familiar plural (*vosotros/-as*) affirmative commands for all verbs, change the -*r* of the infinitive to -*d*.

3. To form polite (formal) singular (*usted*) and plural (*ustedes*) affirmative commands and all negative commands (singular and plural, familiar and polite), use the appropriate form of the present subjunctive. Form the negative in the usual way.

4. To form first person plural (we) commands (let's . . .), use the subjunctive in the affirmative and the negative. In the affirmative, another option is to use *Vamos* + *a* + infinitive.

5. Attach reflexive, indirect, and direct object pronouns directly to the affirmative commands. For example ¡*Háblame!*—Speak to me! For *nosotros/-as* and *vosotros/-as* affirmative commands in reflexive verbs, the last letter is dropped when the reflexive pronouns is attached. For example, ¡*Lavémonos!*—Let's wash ourselves! and ¡*Lavaos!*—Wash yourselves!

In negative commands, place them before the verb in the usual manner. For example ¡*No me hables!*—Don't speak to me!

6. There are several irregular familiar singular affirmative commands:

*tener*—to have: *ten*
*hacer*—to do, make: *haz*
*venir*—to come: *ven*
*decir*—to say, tell: *di*
*poner*—to put, place: *pon*
*ser*—to be: *sé*
*salir*—to leave: *sal*
*ir*—to go: *ve*

## 24. Impersonal Verbs

To conjugate impersonal verbs, i.e., verbs like *gustar*—to be pleasing to, to like, and *doler*—to hurt, use the third person form of the appropriate tense, mood, etc. of the verb and the indirect object pronoun that corresponds to the person, place, or thing affected. Whether to use the singular or plural of the third person form of the verb depends on the number of the items doing the affecting. For example, *Me gusta el Señor González*—I like Mr. González (Mr. González is pleasing to me)/*Me gustan los González*—I like the Gonzálezes.

## 25. Reflexive Verbs

To form reflexive constructions, conjugate the infinitive (without the *-se*) and use the reflexive pronoun that corresponds to the subject. For example:

*lavarse*—to wash oneself
*me lavo*—I wash myself

## 26. Stem-Changing Verbs

There are three kinds of stem-changing verbs.

1. For verbs such as *querer*—to want and *encontrar*—to find, change *e* to *ie* and *o* to *ue* in the stems of all forms except *nosotros, -as* and *vosotros, -as* in the present indicative and present subjunctive. There are no *-ir* verbs in this category.

2. For verbs such as *sentir(se)*—to feel and *dormir*—to sleep, change *e* to *ie* and *o* to *ue* in the exact same places as in the first kind, and change *e* to *i* and *o* to *u* in the *nosotros, -as* and *vosotros, -as* forms of the present subjunctive, in the *él/ella/usted* and *ellos/ellas/ustedes* forms of the preterite, in all forms of the past subjunctive, and in the present participle. Only *-ir* verbs are in this category.

3. For verbs such as *pedir*—to request, change *e* to *i* in all places where any change occurs in the second kind. Only *-ir* verbs are in this category.

## 27. Spelling Changes

To keep pronunciation consistent and to preserve customary spelling in Spanish, some verbs in certain tenses change their spelling. The rules are:

In verbs ending in *-car*, *c* changes to *qu* before *e* to keep the sound hard; e.g., *busqué*—I looked (from *buscar*).

In verbs ending in *-quir*, *qu* changes to *c* before *o* and *a*; e.g., *delinco*—I commit a transgression (from *delinquir*).

In verbs ending in *-zar*, *z* changes to *c* before *e*; *comencé*—I began (from *comenzar*).

In verbs ending in *-gar*, *g* changes to *gu* before *e* to keep the *g* hard; e.g., *pagué*—I paid (from *pagar*).

In verbs ending in a consonant + *-cer/-cir*, *c* changes to *z* before *o* and *a* to keep the sound soft; e.g., *venzo*—I conquer (from *vencer*).

In verbs ending in *-ger/-gir*, *g* changes to *j* before *o* and *a* to keep the sound soft; e.g., *cojo*—I catch (from *coger*).

In verbs ending in *-guir*, *gu* changes to *g* before *o* and *a* to preserve the sound; e.g., *distingo*—I distinguish (from *distinguir*).

In verbs ending in *-guar*, *gu* changes to *gü* before *e* to keep the "gw" sound; e.g., *averigüé*—I ascertained (from *averiguar*).

In verbs ending in *-eer*, the unstressed *i* between vowels becomes a *y;* e.g., *leyó*—he read (from *leer*).

In stem-changing verbs ending in *-eir*, two consecutive *i*'s become one; e.g., *rio*—he laughed (from *reír*).

In stem-changing verbs beginning with a vowel, an *h* must precede the word-initial diphthong or the initial *i* of the diphthong becomes a *y;* e.g., *huelo*—I smell (sense) (from *oler*); *yerro*—I err (from *errar*).

In verbs with stems ending in *ll* or *ñ*, the *i* of the diphthongs *ie* and *ió* disappears; e.g., *bulló*—it boiled (from *bullir*).

# GLOSSARY OF GRAMMATICAL TERMS

**active voice**—voz activa: *a verb form in which the actor (agent) is expressed as the grammatical subject. The girl ate the orange—La chica comió la naranja.*

**adjective**—adjetivo: *a word that describes a noun; e.g., pretty—bonita.*

**adverb**—adverbio: *a word that describes verbs, adjectives, or other adverbs; e.g., quickly—rápidamente.*

**agreement**—concordancia: *the modification of words so that they match the words they describe or relate to.*

**auxiliary verb**—verbo auxiliar: *a helping verb used with another verb to express some facet of tense or mood.*

**compound**—compuesto: *verb forms composed of two parts, an auxiliary and a main verb.*

**conditional**—potencial simple: *the mood used for hypothetical (depending on a possible condition or circumstance) statements and questions. I would eat if . . . —Comería si . . .*

**conjugation**—conjugación: *the formation of verbs with their endings; i.e., the finite forms (vs. nonfinite forms such as the infinitive or participle).*

**conjunction**—conjunción: *a word that connects other words and phrases; e.g., and—y.*

**definite article**—artículo definido: *a word linked to a noun indicating it is specific; e.g., the—el (masculine singular).*

**demonstrative**—demostrativo: *words that highlight something referred to; e.g., in this book—este libro, this—este is a demonstrative adjective.*

**diphthong**—diptongo: *a sequence of two vowels that glide together and act as a single sound.*

**direct object**—objeto directo: *the person or thing that receives the action of a verb (accusative)*.

**ending**—desinencia: *the suffixes added to the stem that indicate subject, tense, etc.*

**gender**—género: *grammatical categories for nouns, loosely related to physical gender and/or word ending; Spanish has two, masculine and feminine, e.g., el chico (m), la chica (f)*.

**imperative**—imperativo: *the command form*.

**imperfect**—imperfecto: *the past tense used for ongoing or habitual actions or states; useful for description of events*.

**impersonal verb**—verbo impersonal: *a verb in which the person, place, or thing affected is expressed as the indirect object rather than the subject; e.g., to like (to be pleasing to)—gustar: I like chicken—Me gusta el pollo (the chicken is pleasing to me)*.

**indefinite article**—artículo indefinido: *a word linked to a noun indicating that it is nonspecific; e.g., a/an—un (masculine singular)*.

**indicative**—indicativo: *the mood used for factual or objective statements and questions*.

**indirect object**—objeto indirecto: *the person or thing that receives the action of the direct object and/or is the object of a preposition (dative)*.

**infinitive**—infinitivo: *the basic form of a verb found in the dictionary that does not specify the subject (person or number), tense, or mood; e.g., to speak—hablar*.

**mood**—modo: *the attitude toward what is expressed by the verb*.

**noun**—sustantivo: *a word referring to a person, place, or thing; e.g., house—casa*.

**number**—número: *the distinction between singular and plural*.

**participle**—participio: *an unconjugated, unchanging verb form often used with auxiliary verbs to form compound verb forms; e.g., present and past participles: eating/eaten—comiendo/comido.*

**passive voice**—voz pasiva: *a verb form in which the recipient of the action is expressed as the grammatical subject. The orange was eaten by the girl—La naranja fue comida por la chica.*

**perfect**—perfecto: *verb forms used for actions or states that are already completed. I have eaten—He comido.*

**person**—persona: *the grammatical category that distinguishes between the speaker (first person), the person spoken to (second person), and the people and things spoken about (third person); often applies to pronouns and verbs.*

**pluperfect**—pluscuamperfecto: *the past perfect using the imperfect of haber—to have (in either the indicative or the subjunctive) plus the past participle.*

**possessive**—posesivo: *indicates ownership; e.g., my—mi is a possessive pronoun (genitive).*

**predicate**—predicado: *the part of the sentence containing the verb and expressing the action or state of the subject.*

**preposition**—preposición: *a word (often as part of a phrase) that expresses spatial, temporal, and other relationships; e.g., on—en.*

**preterite**—pretérito: *the past tense used for completed actions or states; useful for narration of events.*

**progressive**—progresivo: *verb form used for actions that are ongoing. I am eating—Estoy comiendo.*

**pronoun**—pronombre: *a word taking the place of a noun; e.g., personal or demonstrative.*

**reflexive verb**—verbo reflexivo: *a verb whose action reflects back to the subject; e.g., to wash oneself—lavarse.*

**simple**—simple: *one-word verb forms conjugated by adding endings to a stem.*

**stem or root**—raíz: *the part of the infinitive that does not change during the conjugation of regular verbs formed by dropping -ar, -er; or -ir; e.g., habl- in hablar.*

**subject**—sujeto: *the person, place, or thing performing the action of the verb or being in the state described by it (nominative).*

**subjunctive**—subjuntivo: *the mood used for nonfactual or subjective statements or questions.*

**tense**—tiempo: *the time of an action or state, i.e., past, present, future.*

**verb**—verbo: *a word expressing an action or state; e.g., (to) walk—caminar.*